A STRATEGIC GUIDE TO FOOTBALL

A Strategic Guide
to Football

Wesley C Zaba

ISBN: 1505862329
ISBN 13: 9781505862324
Library of Congress Control Number: 2015901503
CreateSpace Independent Publishing Platform
North Charleston, South Carolina

AUTHOR BIOGRAPHY

WESLEY ZABA, AUTHOR of *A Strategic Guide to Football*, is a licensed attorney, real estate broker, and real estate instructor. He has taught several different classes and seminars covering everything from estate planning and real estate to statistical analysis. He also belongs to several bar associations, real estate clubs, and investment groups. Prior to authoring this book, he published three articles on statistical analysis and calculations, and has consulted with several football teams to discuss the framework and implementation of the strategies covered in this book.

To contact the author regarding questions, comments, or thoughts, feel free to email him at footballstrategies@gmail.com. For additional information or to communicate in real-time, you can also follow him on Twitter at @FootballStrats.

TABLE OF CONTENTS

Chapter 1

INTRODUCTION
TO CONCEPTS

FOOTBALL IS A game that has experienced a significant amount of changes over the years. We have seen the league become a predominantly passing league in recent years where running backs have almost become interchangeable, which is much different than how the game was played 50 or even 25 years ago. However, with all of these modifications to the way the game is played and the amount of statistics and analytics that have gone into game planning, there is still one area that is seriously ignored—clock management and in-game strategies. If you do not believe me, just watch a closely contested NFL or college football game any weekend of the year, and on average, a knowledgeable spectator could notice at least seven to eight strategic mistakes that are made...PER GAME! As an advanced time management aficionado, you will likely see closer to 20 to 25 combined mistakes between the teams in that same game, which could end up costing a team a win. If I told a coach that he could improve his chances of winning a given football game by almost 20%, do you think he would listen? As you will see moving forward, this is exactly what clock management and the in-game strategies covered in this book can do for a team properly employing such principles against a team who is not following such strategies.

The purpose of this book is to introduce coaches to the basic clock management principles and other strategic concepts that should be employed by every football team, regardless of level or ability. In the upcoming chapters, we will build on these strategies to demonstrate how to increase your win probability by an even greater amount. Obviously, these concepts will not cause a team to overcome a huge talent gap or change the outcome of a game that would otherwise be a blowout. However, utilizing these concepts on a consistent basis has been shown to increase a team's chances of winning a game against an evenly matched opponent by approximately 20%. In the NFL and NCAA, this could equate to an additional three to four wins per season for the average football team. In high school, this will translate to two to three more wins per season. These additional wins would likely result from closely contested games where your opponent scored a touchdown or field goal in the last minute of the half or game, or you had an opportunity for a last minute drive that ended unsuccessfully.

This begs the question, "If these strategies are so effective, why aren't they currently being used by every team?" Well, there are a couple different answers to this question. First, many coaches are unaware of the proper clock management principles and other strategies contained in this book, in addition to how to properly utilize them. Therefore, they are unable to incorporate them into their in-game analysis and decision-making. Hopefully, after reading this book, more and more coaches will understand the importance of implementing the proper strategies. Second, some coaches are aware of some or most of the principles and concepts incorporated in this book; however, they either refuse or are unable to use them. Let's explore this idea a little further. Many coaches are aware of certain points in a game when they know statistically that they should be "going for it" on fourth down, but instead they choose to punt. The reason for this is because they are afraid that if they are unsuccessful on fourth down, the blame will be placed on them for making an unconventional decision, regardless of whether the decision was statistically the correct or not. Whether you are coaching in high school, college, or the NFL, there are always interested observers judging your performance. These can be general managers, alumni, sport writers, boosters, owners, athletic directors, and so on. And unless these individuals understand why the coach is making a certain decision, these coaches believe that unconventional decisions can hurt them more if they are not successful, than if the coach instead just followed standard operating procedure and makes the conventional decision. Unfortunately, coaches operating in this fashion are costing their teams wins in favor of impressing or not upsetting these outside observers.

Another reason why some coaches have chosen not to implement the strategies in this book is because decades upon decades of coaches have done it differently. Essentially, they believe that all of the greatest college and professional coaches in the past have operated a certain way, and therefore, they must do the same. This is faulty logic for many reasons, but most of all, you are actually doing your team a disservice by not providing them with the best opportunity to win. Think about it. You are asking your players to prepare, condition themselves, workout, learn playbooks, and practice so they give themselves the best chance to succeed. Shouldn't the coach be doing the same as well? New evidence and statistics are constantly developed and evaluated, which provide a perspective into football that may not have existed before. Each and every coach owes it to himself and his team to use the best and most effective strategies to improve the team's chances of winning. As people always say, "Adapt or die." In dealings with coaches from all different levels and sports, it seems that football coaches are most the resistant to change relative to other sports. This is not meant to be an insult, but rather an observation. Look at how much baseball has changed in recent years due to advanced statistics and analysis. Baseball plays previously used significantly, such as the sacrifice bunt or stolen base, are now attempted much less due to a better understanding of the game and what plays increase a team's chances of winning the game. Football coaches generally become very comfortable in their ways and believe what they have learned will continue to work. However, it is important to use all of the information available to you to make the best possible decisions, even if that involves changing your game plan.

Adopting and utilizing the concepts contained in this book will not always be a smooth transition. Just like someone counting cards in blackjack, implementing the proper principles will benefit you in the long run, but there will definitely be some bumps in the road. For example, this book will contain circumstances when a team should go for it on fourth down rather than punt or kick a field goal. Obviously, there will be instances when the team will be unsuccessful and turns the ball over on downs. However, you have to understand the reasoning behind the decision and why it was proper, regardless of the outcome. Most of all, you have to continue abiding by the strategies in this book in order to have the best chance of winning a particular game. People who do not understand statistics or win probability will question coaches' decisions and criticize them when those decisions do not work. You must understand that numbers don't lie. Coaches who utilize the strategies in this book are doing their teams a great service and drastically improving their chances to win every game.

As mentioned before, because of new information and statistics that help people evaluate the game in greater depth, it now appears that even the best coaches of the past have made thousands and thousands of poor decisions. It will be hard for coaches to accept and implement the changes recommended in this book. It means that a lot of what you have learned and practiced for several years, or even decades, has been incorrect and not in the best interest of the team. However, following the strategies of this book will give you the best chance to win any given game, which is ultimately the goal of every team.

The purpose of this chapter is also to provide a framework of what will be covered, as well as introducing certain concepts and terms that will be utilized throughout the book. You will need to understand these concepts as we move forward, so make sure they are reviewed until the words and terms become second nature. This book will provide valuable information, charts, and statistics, as well as the corresponding decision-making techniques for clock management, late-game situations, and specialty plays, in addition to common coaching dilemmas. For example, we will discuss the proper use of time outs, kneel-downs, spiking the ball, and pace of play among many other topics. These plays and decisions will be used in every game by coaches, which is why this book can singularly increase your win total significantly.

CLOCK MANAGEMENT

A large portion of this book will focus on clock management, in addition to several concepts associated with it. Therefore, it is important to understand the goals of clock management before we attack the concepts themselves. The primary goal of clock management is to maximize a team's number of possessions, the expected value of each of possession, and reducing the expected value of the opponent's possessions. We will discuss this in more detail moving forward as this is a central theme of this book. Under proper clock management principles, you are also hoping to increase the length of each possession, and alter your play calling and tempo based on expected value and win probability. Expected value is another topic we will cover in great detail, so it is important to understand the meaning and purpose of this term. Expected value is simply the average value you would expect to experience from a given decision if you repeated the process an infinite number of times and took the average result. This concept is easier to explain using an example, so I will do that as well.

Assume a team has a 45% chance of success when attempting a 2-point conversion. This means that every time that team tries a 2-point conversion, they would expect to score 0.9 points. This is calculated by multiplying your chance of success (0.45) by the amount of points you are awarded when successful (2 points). Obviously, a team cannot actually score 0.9 points; however, according to these statistics, that team would average 0.9 points every time they attempted a 2-point conversion. Another way to explain this concept is that if a team attempted a 2-point conversion 100 times, they would succeed 45 times (45%) for a total of 90 points. Similarly, win probability is the probability that a team will win a game at a given moment, factoring in all of the circumstances affecting the game at that time. This can include the score, possession, time remaining, location on the field, wind, etc. For example, a team may have a 45% chance of winning a particular game prior to the game starting, but almost everything that happens during the game will affect their win probability. Therefore, if they are losing by 3 points in the fourth quarter but have possession on their opponent's 15 yard line with 1 minute left, their chances of winning, or win probability, may be closer to 75%.

There are a couple more concepts that you must become familiar with, which are pace and scoring frequency. Pace is the speed at which the offense is calling and executing their plays. For example, if an offense is snapping the ball within 20 seconds of the end of the previous play, they are operating at a pace twice as fast as an offense that is hiking the ball 40 seconds from the end of the previous play. Pace will be a very important principle as we discuss clock management in more detail. Scoring frequency is the rate at which a team scores. It is very easy to calculate scoring frequency, as you simply take the number of game minutes played in a given period and divide that by the total number of scores during that same period. For example, if a team scored 75 times in an NFL season in 16 games (without overtimes included), that team had a scoring frequency of 12.8 (960 minutes of game time divided by 75 scores). This means that on average, this team scored every 12.8 minutes of game time. To get a more accurate calculation, I generally advise you ignore points and time played in overtime. This can greatly skew the results and cause them to be very misleading. Scoring frequency provides an overview of the average rate at which your team scores. You will also want to perform a separate calculation to determine your scoring frequency when your team is in a fast tempo offense to compare and contrast the results. This will also provide coaches with an estimation of when a team needs to employ a fast tempo in order to allow enough time to score before the end of a half or game. We will discuss this more in detail later in the book.

Many people believe that clock management principles should only be utilized in the last couple minutes of a half or game. This is not entirely accurate. Clock management decisions are not only important in a 2- or 4-minute drill, but also factor into many other plays as well. Depending on the score, time, time outs remaining, possession, and many other factors, clock management principles should be considered in at least 80% of the plays when you are on offense. The clock can be your greatest asset or your worst enemy, and it should be treated as such during a game. We will discuss in the next chapter why this is so important and how these principles can often decide a game.

Special team clock management is also an important factor, which will be discussed in this book. Obviously, every coach is familiar with utilizing the onside kick as a way to "steal" a possession and increase win probability; however, many other special team decisions can factor into a game such as when to punt or fake punt, attempting a field goal, taking an intentional safety, etc. These concepts and decisions will be addressed in the later chapters of this book.

It is important to ensure that the clock management principles and game strategies discussed in this book are practiced by teams before and throughout the season, and not just attempted in the game. Many coaches I have spoken with simply dedicate about an hour a week toward these concepts in addition to introducing them and practicing them in training camp and summer practice. In order to simulate game situations, a scoreboard and play clock should be utilized when practicing these plays or calls, in addition to having extra coaches or volunteers act as referees. As discussed before, a team's win percentage can change in a matter of seconds and with every single play, so a team must be able to adapt in order to take advantage of these situations. Additionally, executing proper clock management procedures requires both the coaches and players to understand not only the concepts and principles, but the theories and calculations behind them. Players do not necessarily need to be able to calculate the statistics associated with these strategies, but it is important to understand the strategies so they can comprehend why certain actions or plays are being called and at what pace they are expected to play.

If you remember, clock management principles affect about 80% of plays in a game. There are a significant amount of factors that must be considered and calculated within a few seconds of the previous play ending in order to determine the correct decision for the next play. These decisions can be whether to go for it or kick, what pace should be used, and what type of play should be called, among several others. This is why I believe it is very important for each team to employ a strategic assistant who focuses exclusively on the concepts and principles within this book. No other coach has the time and knowledge to do so, unless he has worked in a similar capacity before. It is also important to have the proper charts, tables, and software programs, which can significantly streamline the process for these assistants. I am in complete shock that every NFL, college, and high school team does not have one of these strategic assistants working for them. If you think of how many other coaches are present on the sidelines, it is really quite surprising.

According to statistical data from the last three NFL seasons, an offense has a correlation factor of approximately 0.431, meaning that during an average NFL game, the offense contributes about 43.1% to whether a team wins that particular game. If you take those statistics one step further, the wide receivers and running backs are each responsible for approximately 16% of the productivity of the offense, meaning that wide receivers and running backs each contribute to approximately 6.8% of the overall game. Previously, I had mentioned that a strategic assistant to the head coach could improve a team's chances to win a particular game by up to 20% if the proper methods and strategies contained in this book are implemented in each game. Why then, are football programs paying hundreds of thousands of dollars to positional coaches such as running backs coaches, defensive backs coaches, wide receivers coaches, and so on, without hiring a special strategic assistant, who can impact the game even more than any of those position coaches? No disrespect is meant to these other coaching positions, but it is important to understand the significance of having a strategic assistant to advise the head coach of the appropriate decisions based on the calculations.

Special strategic assistants should also be responsible for ensuring the game and play clocks stop and start at the appropriate time. I cannot tell you how many times I have been watching football games and an extra 2 to 5 seconds have run off the clock unnecessarily because it was not stopped at the appropriate time. For example, the Carolina Panthers hosted the New England Patriots in Week 11 of the 2013 season. This game was remembered for a controversial finish, but that was only part of the story. Carolina scored a touchdown late in the fourth quarter to take the lead by 4 points, leaving :59 on the clock for Tom Brady and the Patriots. However, there actually should have been more time remaining on the clock. If you reviewed that play, the receiver for the Panthers, Ted Ginn Jr., crossed the goal line with approximately 1:04 remaining, but the clock operator was slow to stop the clock, whether intentionally or unintentionally. So do you think five seconds really matter? Well they could have. The Patriots drove down to the Panthers 18 yard line on the ensuing drive, where, with only three seconds left, Brady had to throw a risky do-or-die pass into the end zone, which was ultimately intercepted. However, if the Patriots would have had the 5 additional seconds on the clock, which they should have, a lot more options would have been available to them as they could have likely had enough time for a second play, possibly preventing Brady from having to throw the risky pass. We will never know what could have happened, but this should be a lesson that having a strategic assistant to the head coach who also keeps his focus on the clock can prove to be a huge benefit. Unfortunately, incorrect clockwork is a normal occurrence that happens almost every week, so coaches should always have someone tracking the game clock.

Additionally, very few teams, if any, keep clock management statistics in order to track the effectiveness of their decisions. Mostly this is because coaches believe that these strategic concepts are of minor importance to a specific game. However, as described above, you can see that it can be the most important aspect of a game. Clock management decisions become exponentially more important in close games because one play or an extra 10 seconds on the clock can be the difference between winning and losing. It is important for all coaches to use the information available to make the proper decisions throughout a particular game. In the upcoming chapters, you will be introduced to the individual concepts and principles to be utilized no matter what level you are coaching.

WIN PROBABILITY

Earlier in the introduction, we briefly discussed win probability. Again, win probability is the percentage chance that a team will win a game at a given moment in time, factoring in all of the circumstances affecting the game at that point. This is a very important concept and has its own section dedicated to it because this is the statistic that should drive the decision-making discussed in this book, along with any other decisions a coach makes during a game. Your goal throughout a game is to increase this figure as much as possible until the game is over. Win probability can be calculated at any point in a game, or even before a game has started. Prior to the beginning of the game, teams generally do not have an equal chance of winning. One team is usually favored, meaning that they have a greater chance of winning that game, and this can be based on talent, home-field advantage, injuries, weather conditions, etc. Only about 2 to 4% of games are truly even games where each team has an equal probability of winning.

Obviously, with sports betting lines offered almost everywhere nowadays, it can be rather easy to determine which team is the favorite in college and NFL games. You can simply look in your local newspaper or online to check the latest line for a game. For example, if a team is listed at -8, it means that they are an 8 point favorite in the game and the linemakers believe they will win the game by 8 points. Another way to view this is to prorate spread throughout the quarters. For the purposes of calculating win probability, if a team is an 8-point favorite, you can assume the favorite should win each quarter by 2 points. Obviously it does not usually happen this way, and this is not exactly accurate for reasons we will discuss later, but this can give coaches a running total to assist in calculations at the end of each quarter. Under this prorated assumption, if the game is tied at halftime, the team favored by 8 points before the game is now a 4-point favorite to win the game because there are only two quarters remaining, and they are favored by 2 points each quarter. Alternatively, if the underdog (the team that is not favored) is leading by 4 points at half, it can be assumed that each team has an equal chance of winning the game because the favored team is expected to outscore the underdog by 4 points in the second half. This type of analysis can be very important in determining win probability as the game is progressing, and the coaches must be ready to alter their in-game decisions based on the often-changing win probability.

Another question coaches often ask is, "How do I evaluate which team is favored if the teams compete at the high school level or below?" Obviously, there are no betting lines set for these games, so it can be a little more difficult and time-consuming. One way that coaches evaluate this situation is by loss addition. Under this formula, you take the record for each team competing in the game, calculate the total amount of losses of each team's previous opponents, and add those to each team's records. At that point, whoever has the best modified record, by winning percentage, would be favored. For example, assume Team A is 3–0 and Team B is 2–1. On the surface it would look like Team A is favored. However, now assume that Team A's previous opponents currently have a record of 1–8. Adjusting for the previous opponent's records, Team A would now have a modified record of 3–8. Let's also assume that Team B's opponents currently have a record of 5–4, making Team B's modified record 2–5. Under this formula, Team A would have a modified winning percentage of 0.273, while Team B would have a modified winning percentage of 0.286. Therefore, Team B would actually be favored in this game because of the difference in the modified records and the higher winning percentage. Obviously, this mathematical formula is not foolproof and cannot be used in every circumstance, such as the first game of the season, but it does provide more in-depth analysis than simply comparing the two teams' records, which can be deceiving. This method also does not provide an amount by which a team is favored, but again, certain assumptions can be made to arrive at an approximate value. The strategic assistant will want to know or calculate the spread before the game starts because it will impact a variety of different calculations and decisions to be made during the game.

As you will see in the next chapter, the win probability at each given moment will affect many of the decisions that a coach makes, such as choosing at what pace to operate. The team with the lead will see its win probability increase as the game approaches the final whistle, with all other factors remaining the same. This is because the less time that is remaining in the game, fewer plays can be run, and therefore, it is less likely that the lead will change. This concept will be covered in greater detail in the next chapter, and you will see how to make the correct corresponding decisions. Additionally, the importance of points and drives increases as the game proceeds. For example, if Team A is losing by 7 points in the first quarter and Team A has possession of the ball at their own 35 yard line on first down, the win probability for Team A is approximately 32.4%. This means that as of that point, Team A has a 32.4% chance of winning this game. If the ball is then advanced to the opponent's 35 yard line, the win probability of Team A now increases to 38.2%, which is an increase of 5.8%. However, if we take those same circumstances, except now assume the game is in the fourth quarter, Team A will have a 10.7% chance of winning the game from their own 35 yard line, and a 28.8% chance of winning from their opponent's 35 yard line. This is now an increase of 18.1% for the exact same situation, except for the amount of time remaining in the game. This demonstrates the increased significance of drives and possessions as the game proceeds because, in the example above, Team A still has plenty of time to overcome the deficit in the first quarter while they have very little time to do so in the fourth quarter. Therefore, clock management and other strategic decisions become more important as the game progresses, especially in the fourth quarter and overtime.

Another assumption made while calculating win probability is that the number of possessions Team A will have in a game will be within one of the number of possessions Team B will have, barring the kicking team's recovery of an onside kick. A team cannot have more possessions than their opponent in each half because each team will be required to kick-off in one of the halves, so they will never have more possessions than their opponent in that half, again, barring the recovery of an onside kick. Therefore, each team's goal should be to have one more possession than their opponent at the end of every game, unless they have scored on their last possession with the clock winding down, leaving the opponent little or no time left on the clock. If a team can successfully achieve this goal, they will increase their chances of winning by 7 to 11% depending on the number of possessions in that game. The question then becomes "How can a team accomplish that?" First of all, a team always wants to have the last possession of the first half, discounting any kneel-down possessions of their opponent. Typically, a coach will want to alter the pace of his team's possessions based on the time remaining on the clock. Starting with about 8 to 10 minutes left in the second quarter, the coach's decisions and strategies should not only be governed by attempting to score points, but also by having the last possession of the half. We will discuss this further in the next chapter when we cover proper pace.

Finally, there are many phrases in football circles that, unfortunately, have become commonplace despite being statistically incorrect. For example, how many times have you heard someone say, "You never take points off the board" or "You are supposed to go for the win on the road and the tie at home"? The goal under the win probability theory is to score as many points as possible, which will give you the greatest possible chance of winning. For example, let's assume an NFL team is on offense and it is 4th and 4 from their opponent's 10 yard line. The offense lines up and kicks the field goal, which is successful; however, the defense was offside. Assuming that time is not a factor, the offense's two choices are now to decline the penalty and take the 3 points, or accept the penalty, which would place the ball at the 5 yard line with a first down. Conventional thinking would be to take the points, because after all, you are not supposed to take points off the board. The expected value of that decision, without factoring in the subsequent kickoff, is simply the 3 points the offense is guaranteed if they select this option. However, what happens if the penalty is accepted? Under this alternative, the offense will have first and goal from the 5 yard line, which has an expected value of almost 5.5 points. Therefore, according to these statistics, if the offense accepts the penalty, their expected value would increase by approximately 2.5 points, thereby increasing their win probability. This is how expected value is used to improve win probability. After all, the ultimate goal of all coaching decisions made during a game is to increase a team's win probability whenever possible.

Another issue to consider is the timing of the decision. As stated before, the goal under the win probability theory is to score as many points as possible per possession, which will directly increase your win probability.

However, what if we assume the same situation stated in the previous paragraph if there were only 15 seconds remaining in the game and the offense was down 2 points prior to the play? Obviously, at that point, maximizing points is not the goal offense, but rather scoring enough to win the game. Under these circumstances, it would be wiser to decline the penalty, take the 3 points, and proceed with the lead even though this goes against the expected value theory. In situations such as this, the analysis becomes much more intensive as the strategic assistant must be able to calculate the win probability of declining the penalty and taking the lead versus accepting the penalty and retaining possession. Again, this analysis must be done in a matter of seconds, which further emphasizes the importance of having this assistant on staff because no other coach will have the knowledge and resources to make such a decision in a short enough period.

Another old adage I would like to address is the theory of going for the win on the road versus going for the tie at home. The basis of this theory is correct, even if the resulting statement is not. This theory is based on the concept that a home team is more likely to win a given game because they are playing on their home field. Therefore, if the home team is able to tie the game at the end of regulation, they will be more likely to win it in overtime than the visiting team because they are favored. Again, if a team is favored, they will statistically be the next team to score because they are assumed to be the better team. Conversely, the opposite would be true for the visiting team, and assuming that the visiting team is not favored, they would be more likely to lose should the game proceed to overtime. As a result, this theory states that the visiting team should go for the win in regulation because they will be an underdog in ovetime.

As I mentioned, the underlying assumption is correct that the favored team should secure the tie because they are more likely to win in overtime due the fact that they are the better team, barring any circumstances that occurred during the game that may affect their ability to win the game, such as a significant injury. Therefore, the conclusion should state that the favored team should go for the tie while the underdog should be more aggressive in attempting to secure the win in regulation. This differs from the old adage because the home team is not always favored. Last season, the home team in the NFL was the underdog approximately 38% of the time, and during these games, the conventional wisdom stating that the home team should go for the tie would be incorrect. Again, this is another instance where it is important to understand and be honest about the likelihood of a team succeeding in a particular game because this will assist in arriving at the correct decision.

On the internet, there are several sites that provide a win probability calculator where you can enter certain information such as score, time remaining in the game, possession, field position, down and distance, etc., and it will provide the win probability at that given time based on the circumstances inputted. However, you must be careful if you rely too heavily on these calculators. First off, each of these different calculators uses a slightly different underlying formula to compute the win probability, so they will not all be consistent with each other. Second, there are other factors that must be considered other than those referenced above when determining win probability, such as weather, in-game injuries, and so on. Finally, some of the win probability calculators do not take into account the difference in talent between the two teams playing. These formulas assume that each game contains two teams that are evenly matched, and therefore, each have an identical talent level. However, as we discussed earlier, you must be aware of which team is favored in a given game and continue to incorporate that data into your calculations. This cannot be overstated because this information can drastically alter win probabilities, especially if there is a large talent gap between the teams.

For example, let's assume Team A is a 14-point underdog in a particular game but is leading by 6 points at halftime. Our previous analysis based on handicapping a team would indicate that the favorite, Team B, will outscore Team A by 7 points in the second half, and thus may still be favored to win the game even though they are losing at halftime. However, certain win probability calculators will not take the spread into account and will estimate that Team A has a 72% chance of winning the game based solely on the score and time remaining. Therefore, you must always be sure to include all relevant information in win probability calculations.

In the coming chapters, we are going to delve a little deeper into some of the concepts we touched on in this chapter and further explain some of the statistics and analysis behind such concepts, which will allow coaches to make the appropriate decisions. We will also introduce some additional strategies and principles that will hopefully provide a deeper understanding of how a coaching staff should be preparing and operating during a game. Again, this chapter was meant to be an introduction or preliminary look into clock management and other in-game strategies, but it is only a foundation. If any of these concepts or ideas still seem foreign to you, or if you do not fully understand them, please be sure to review them or read over this chapter again.

It is essential that terms such as win probability and expected value are understood because these will provide a basis for many of the future strategies and coaching decisions covered in this book. Otherwise, if you are able to comprehend the basic concepts discussed thus far, we can now begin moving into more advanced concepts. These concepts will include clock management and the different paces in which an offense can operate. We will also cover fourth down decisions, such as when the statistics show that an offense should go for it, kick a field goal, or punt. Additionally, we will look into many late-game plays such as taking a knee, spiking the ball, and certain desperation plays such as the Hail Mary pass or lateral plays. Finally, we will cover certain special teams plays, and of course, no clock management book would be complete without a chapter covering when time-outs should be called by coaches both on offense and defense.

CHAPTER 1 SUMMARY

- There are commonly 20 to 25 combined strategic mistakes committed in an average NFL or college game.
- Abiding by the principles and concepts in this book can increase a team's chances of winning by up to 20%.
- The primary goal of clock management is to maximize the expected value of each of your teams' possessions and reduce the amount of your opponents' possessions.
- Expected value is the average net points a team would expect to experience from a given decision if you repeated the process an infinite number of times.
- Win probability is the percentage chance a team will win a game at a given moment, factoring in all of the circumstances at that point in the game. This calculation should be performed constantly throughout the game.
- Pace is the speed at which an offense is operating, measured by the amount of time between snaps.
- Scoring frequency is the rate at which a team scores, which is calculated by dividing the number of game minutes played by the total number of scores during that period.
- Clock management decisions factor into a majority of plays in a given game, not just in the last 2 or 4 minutes of a half.
- Given the amount of clock management and strategic decisions that must be made during the course of a game, teams should employ a strategic assistant to the head coach to calculate and monitor game trends and provide the required information to the head coach or play caller.
- Coaches must reevaluate many of the decisions they have been making in order to ensure they are the statistically correct decisions.

Chapter 2

PACE OF PLAY

IN THE INTRODUCTION, we covered some of the basic principles of clock management, but in this chapter, we are going to discuss one of the most important clock management strategies and demonstrate how it can change the course of the game. If you remember from the previous chapter, pace is defined as the speed at which the offense is calling and executing their plays. It can be measured by the amount of time that elapses from when the previous play concludes to when the ball is snapped, beginning the following play. The purpose of this chapter is to educate coaches on the different paces that exist in football and discuss how to determine the proper pace that a team should be using when they are on offense. There are generally five paces that are used in football, and we are going to define each one of them so that coaches can be familiar with each of them.

The pace that most people are familiar with is called normal pace. This is when an offense is not attempting to run down the game clock or preserve time. The primary goal of an offense operating at this pace is to work toward scoring the maximum amount of points on a particular drive, regardless of the amount of time it takes. This if often referred to as Pace Three. Interestingly, as you will soon learn, this is one of the lesser-used paces under proper clock management principles.

The next pace we will cover is the hurry-up offense, which is considered Pace Four. Under this pace, the goal of the offense is to score as many points as possible on a given drive, while also minimizing the time it takes to do so. The effort to preserve as much time as possible is generally a secondary goal of this pace; however, there will be an added benefit in doing so as will be demonstrated shortly. Despite the increased pace of the offense, this is usually not the offense to be used in the 2-minute drill late in the game when a team needs to score in a very short period of time. Instead, Pace Five would be the appropriate pace for that situation

When an offense is operating in Pace Five, the primary objective is to move the ball quickly down the field while attempting to score. Scoring can be the more important element of this pace, but doing so as quickly as possible can be equally or more significant. This pace is utilized when attempting a drive in the last minute or two of the half or game, when a touchdown or field goal may be necessary. Under this pace, all efforts should be made to preserve the time on the game clock even at the expense of potentially gaining additional yards. For example, if you are trailing by 2 points with possession of the ball on your own 20 yard line with :45 remaining in the game, the clock is your primary obstacle. In this scenario, a team would willingly forego a 3 to 5 yard gain where the ball carrier is tackled in-bounds and the game clock continues to run, in favor of an incomplete pass, which would not gain any yardage, but would stop the clock. Again, the primary goal is to preserve enough time to allow the offense to score. That is the major difference between Pace Four and Five. In Pace Four, you would prefer the small gain discussed in the previous example, as the primary objective is to score, while conserving time is a secondary goal.

On the other end of the spectrum is the slowest pace, called the "max slow down," or Pace One. While operating in this pace, the primary objective of the offense is to remove as much time from the game clock as possible. In this pace, first downs are usually more important than scoring, as you are often trying to protect a lead late in the game or minimize the amount of time left on the clock for your opponent to score. In Pace One, scoring can be a secondary objective, or in some instances, may not be a goal of the offense at all. For example, if an offense team is winning by 1 point and has the ball with less than 2 minutes left, the offense would be operating in Pace One with the primary goal being for the offense to run out the clock. Scoring would be completely unnecessary in this situation and could even be a detriment, as that would allow the opposition to tie the game with a touchdown and a 2-point conversion as we will discuss later in this book. Therefore, in this situation, draining the clock of all remaining time would be the primary goal of the offense, while scoring would not necessarily be an objective at all.

Finally, Pace Two, or "slow-down pace" is when an offense is trying to score as many points as possible on a particular drive or possession, but is also trying to utilize as much time as possible. This will reduce the amount of time remaining in the game for the opponent to change the outcome and can optimize a team's chances of winning, which we will cover later in this chapter. As we progress, we will provide information on how to identify at which pace an offense should be operating and the benefits of doing so. Obviously, the primary goal of any football decision is to increase a team's chances to win that particular game, and the same is true when identifying which pace an offense should be utilizing.

The proper pace of an offense is usually determined by a general concept. How many times have you been thinking after a loss, "What if we had time for a couple more plays" or "We left our opponent too much time after we scored"? The purpose of operating at the correct pace is to leave your opponents asking themselves those exact questions. The underlying concept that dictates the pace of your offense states that, all else being equal, if your win probability is less than 50%, you should be in a hurry-up offense, Pace Four or Five, and if your win probability is more than 50%, you should be in a slow-down offense, Pace One or Two. If, and only if, your win probability is at 50% should you be in a normal paced offense. The reason for this is simple. If an offense is operating in a hurry-up pace, more plays will be run in that game, which will result in a greater amount of points that will be scored. Conversely, if an offense is operating in a slow-down pace, less plays are run in a game, and on average, a fewer amount of points will be scored in the remainder of the game.

In an average NFL game, 0.37 points are scored every play. This means that, on average, for every 100 plays run in the NFL, the teams will combine for 37 points. Additionally, the more points that are scored in a game increases the chances of a lead change. To illustrate this point, let's assume Team A is down by 7 points in a particular game. If there are a combined 10 more points scored in this game, with all else being equal, Team A's win probability would be 17%. However, if there were 20 more total points scored in this hypothetical game, Team A's win probability would be 22%, and it would increase even further to 28% if there were 30 more points scored. The purpose of this example is to demonstrate that the more points that are scored in the remainder of a given game, there is a greater chance that there will be at least one lead change, so this would benefit the team trailing at that point because they would need at least one lead change in order to win the game. Therefore, if a team's win probability is less than 50%, that team's objective should be to speed up the game in order to increase the number of plays in the remainder of the game. This will, in turn, increase the amount of points scored, thereby increasing that team's win probability. As a result of this analysis, a team with a win probability of less than 50% should typically be operating their offense in Pace Four for the reasons described herein.

On the other hand, if a team's win probability is greater than 50% at any point in the game, the opposite would be true, and the offense should be operating in Pace Two in order to drain time from the game clock while still attempting to score as many points as possible. Utilizing more time will reduce the total number of plays run during the remainder game, which will reduce the total amount of points scored, and increase that team's win probability. This will offer them the greatest opportunity to protect the lead and win the game.

This is an example of why a coach must always be aware of their team's win probability, which can change in an instant. Assuming Team A is winning by 3 points and has a corresponding win probability over 50%, they would be operating in Pace Two when they had possession as discussed above. However, if Team B forced a punt and scored a touchdown on their next possession, thereby taking a 4-point lead, Team A may now have a win probability of less than 50%, which would dictate operating their offense in Pace Four to increase the combined scoring of the teams. This is another reason why it may be necessary to have a strategic assistance to the head coach who is always aware of the team's estimated win probability, and who can communicate this information to the offensive coordinator (or other play caller) and quarterback. Many head coaches have way too much information to process to be saddled with the additional responsibility of calculating win probability on a regular basis.

As mentioned before, if a team's win probability is above or below 50%, they should generally be in Pace Two or Four. However, this is independent of the time remaining on the game clock, and therefore, there are some exceptions. One of the primary objectives of proper clock management is to maximize a team's number of possessions. In each game, assuming there are no onside kicks recovered by the kicking team, either each team will have an equal number of possessions, or one team will have one extra possession. Every team's goal for each game should be to have one more "effective possession" than your opponent. The only way to accomplish this is to have the last possession of each half in every single game. Obviously, this is not realistic because that is almost impossible to accomplish, but we will cover the acceptable range later in this book. The reason I use the term "effective possession" is because there will be situations where one team has the last possession of the half, but there may not be adequate time to accomplish anything.

For example, if Team A scores a touchdown with 2 seconds remaining in the first half, they are considered to have the last effective possession of the half, even though Team B will receive the subsequent kickoff and technically have possession when the half expires. In this situation, Team B will have too little time to score, so it does not constitute an effective possession. I generally define an effective possession as a possession where the offense has a reasonably adequate chance of obtaining a scoring opportunity. It does not necessarily have to be a high-percentage opportunity, and points do not have to be scored to constitute an effective possession, but rather, it is simply a possession where a reasonable chance of scoring exists. I understand that is a subjective definition; however, it generally becomes a judgment call of the strategic assistant of what constitutes an effective possession. Additionally, possessions that include kneel-downs to end the half, or when the game clock expires on a change of possession, such as a punt or kickoff, do not constitute effective possessions.

If a team is able to obtain an extra possession, as is the goal every game, the question then becomes how much of an advantage would an extra effective possession provide? On average, an NFL team scores 1.92 points per possession. This means that if a team were able to secure one more effective possession than their opponent each game, they could increase their scoring by 1.92 points per game. How much of a difference would 1.92 points make in an NFL game? First, let's take a look at the average scoring differential in NFL games. Looking at game data from the previous 10 NFL seasons, about 5.5% of games went to overtime, with approximately 0.2% of games ending in a tie. Additionally, 4.27% of games were decided by 1 point, and 3.74% were decided by 2 points. Assuming that a team would win roughly half of the games decided by 1 or 2 points without the extra possession, and accounting for the games which end regulation in a tie, an additional 2 points (rounding up from 1.92 points) could be the difference between winning and losing in over 9.5% of games in the NFL. Stated another way, if a team had one extra effective possession in each game during the regular season, on average, that team could win an additional 1.5 games per season!

In an average NFL game, each team typically has approximately 11 to 12 effective possessions. The average possession in the first and third quarter will last about 3.41 minutes, and the average possession in the second and fourth quarters will last 2.47 minutes based on the same historical data. This reduction of average time of possession in the second and fourth quarters is the result of the change in clock stoppage rules in those quarters and the additional time-outs that are utilized by each team. College and high school games typically have slightly more possessions and each possession lasts a little longer on average because of the stoppage of time on first downs.

Why are we discussing these numbers? Because in order to have the last possession in each half, a team needs adequate planning and calculating. Usually, I recommend planning for the last possession of the half with approximately 8 to 10 minutes left in the second or fourth quarter, depending on who has possession of the ball at that time, and where the ball is located in the field. Obviously, when a team is on offense, they have much more control over how much time is utilized between and during each play, and therefore, they can better prepare to have the last possession of the half. A strategic assistant will use these average times of possession in order to make the appropriate decisions for the remainder of the half, with the goal of having the last effective possession. The time remaining in the half may also require a coach to abandon the proper pace of play based on win probability, as discussed previously, in order to pursue the final possession. For instance, assume Team A is losing by 10 points and has a win probability of 25%. Team A also has possession of the ball on their own 20 yard line with 4:02 left in the first half. Although the pace analysis states that Team A's win probability is below 50%, and therefore they should be operating in Pace Four, Team A should actually be operating in Pace Two based on the time remaining in the half. The goal of having the final effective possession is more important, and therefore supersedes the pace analysis detailed above.

Furthermore, because the average possession in the second and fourth quarters lasts only 2.47 minutes, in order to utilize the entire amount, or effective entire amount, of the remaining 4:02, that team must operate at a slowed pace, Pace Two, to increase their odds of doing so. In all levels of football, too little emphasis is placed on having the last possession of each half and coaches often consider this goal much later than they should. Based on recent data and discussions, it appears most coaches begin planning for the last possession of the half or game with anywhere from 2 to 4 minutes remaining in the half. By this time, a proper clock management expert will have already been planning for over 5 minutes, and should be several steps ahead of the average coach.

Think about the statistics. As stated earlier, having one more effective possession than your opponent can increase your chances of winning by 9.5%. However, if a team does not employ proper clock management principles, and each team has the last possession of one of the halves, their chances of winning will decrease by 8% versus utilizing these techniques. Even worse, if an opponent has one more possession than you in a given game, which statistically will occur an average of one out of every four games without either team using these strategies, then their chance of winning can increase by the same 9.5%, meaning that you have just reduced your chances of winning by a total of 19% compared to if you had the additional possession! This should demonstrate the importance of every team understanding and utilizing the proper pace in order to achieve an extra effective possession in each game.

Again, win probability needs to be reevaluated on a regular basis. At any point during a game, the strategic assistant should be able to provide an accurate win probability for their team. Typically, I recommend recalculating win probability after each score, change of possession, or when an offense gains more than 20 yards on a play. Otherwise, it should be done after every 3 minutes of game time. This should provide an adequately accurate estimation of win probability at any point in the game. Additionally, as the game progresses closer to its conclusion, win probability must be calculated more often because it becomes increasingly important and can change drastically at any given moment in a close game. For example, I typically recalculate win probability after every other play once the fourth quarter begins, and after every play in the last 5 minutes of a game.

AVERAGE PACE GRAPH

When a team has the final possession of the half or game, they should use additional analysis to determine the proper pace at which the offense should be operating. As stated earlier in this chapter, the pace of a team's last possession of the half or game may contradict everything discussed earlier due to the importance or time implications of that drive. If a team has one final possession in the half or game, or they would like it to be the last possession, one way to proceed is through an average pace graph. This is a relatively simple concept that can be incredibly helpful. For example, if a team has the ball on their own 40 yard line with 3:15 remaining in the game and trailing by 4 points, the offense's obvious objective is to score a touchdown. However, they would also like to do so in the appropriate timeframe so their opponent does not have enough time to drive down and score on the ensuing drive. This graph can also be used for a field goal if that is all that is necessary to win/tie the game. In order to utilize this concept, a team will need to determine how many yards they will need to gain per minute, which can simply be done by dividing the amount of yards needed by the amount of minutes remaining (including seconds). The amount of yards a team needs to gain can be the yardage between the line of scrimmage and the opponent's end zone, or the yardage between the line of scrimmage and the yard line the offense would need to attain in order to give their field goal kicker a reasonable opportunity to tie or win the game.

Using the previous example, the offense would need to gain 60 yards in 3.25 minutes (remember to convert seconds to proper decimal form), which means they would need to gain approximately 18.46 yards per minute, or about 0.31 yards every second (yards needed divided by seconds remaining). When conducting this analysis, be sure there is also enough time remaining if an extra play is needed, such as setting up for a last second field goal. If a field goal is the objective, the offense needs to ensure they either have a time-out remaining to stop the clock and set up the field goal unit, or there is adequate time to have the proper unit set up for such a play. For instance, if it takes 25 seconds from the conclusion of the previous play to get the field goal unit on the field and snap the ball, and the offense has no time-outs remaining, the coach would need to subtract 25 seconds from the time remaining in the calculation above in order to calculate the proper average pace.

As a general rule, if the average pace calculation results in the offense needing to gain at or below 5 yards per min, the offense should be in Pace One, or maximum slow down. Otherwise, it will be virtually impossible to avoid leaving time remaining on the clock for the other team to have an ensuing opportunity to score. On the other hand, if the offense needs to gain greater than or equal to 35 yards per minute in this final drive, they will almost certainly be in Pace Five, or maximum fast-paced, which hopefully will allow the offense enough time to gain enough yards as needed. Typically, an offense needing 15 to 20 yards per minute will operate in a Pace Three offense, which is a normal pace. Refer to the following graph for a recommended breakdown of the pace based on the average yards per minute a team must gain to reach their goal. Again, be sure you recalculate this figure after every play because if there is a significant change in circumstances, such as a large gain or sack, the result of this calculation could be substantially different and the pace may need to be modified as well.

PACE	YARDS PER MINUTES
Pace One: Maximum Slow-Paced Offense	Less than 5
Pace Two: Slow-Paced Offense	5 to 14
Pace Three: Normal Offense	15 to 23
Pace Four: Fast-Paced Offense	24 to 34
Pace Five: Maximum Fast-Paced Offense	35+

We have covered a great deal about pace of play in this chapter; however, these concepts and strategies will only work if everybody is on the same page, including the offense and coaching staff. If a team is operating in Pace Four or Pace Five, the entire offense needs to be aware of this, because in order to operate at this pace, the offense must be able and willing to get to the huddle or line of scrimmage in a short time following the previous play. Typically, the strategic assistant will signal to indicate to the quarterback and play caller the proper pace in which to operate, and this information should be passed along to the offensive players on the field.

Under normal circumstances, the offensive coordinator, or whoever is calling the plays for the offense, will need to get the play call relayed much sooner for Pace Four and Five offenses, and he should be thinking one to two plays ahead at all times in order to accomplish this. Therefore, it is important that the strategic assistant is calculating and determining the proper pace, and that this is communicated to the necessary parties. I recommend that the strategic assistant be located on the sideline about 10 to 15 yards behind the line of scrimmage. This will usually provide adequate space from other individuals so he/she is not covered by a crowd, and is clearly visible to players on the field, coaches on the field and sideline, as well as any staff members sitting in the press box.

Another recommendation I have for offensive play callers, in order to make their job easier, is to have different play sheets for different paces. I am not recommending that a coach should have five different play sheets; however, he could have three different sheets: one for a fast, hurry-up offense, Paces Four and Five, one for a normal paced offense, Pace Three, and one for a slow-down offense, Paces One and Two. This will eliminate the time that this coach will have to peruse plays in order to find the appropriate one. As a general rule, a fast-paced or hurry-up offensive play sheet could have plays that end near the sideline in order to stop the clock and save time, and will also likely have more passes than run plays, given that when a team is in a hurry-up offense, they are usually trying to gain larger chunks of yardage in a shorter period of time. Similarly, the play sheet for the slow-down offense would contain more runs and shorter, higher-percentage passes, which will result in the clock continuing to run more often.

Meanwhile, a normal-paced play sheet will have an even split of runs and passes and can contain plays that will likely end near the sideline or in the middle if the field. Also, plays can appear on more than one play sheet if they meet multiple criteria. For instance, if you have a draw play, this could appear on all three sheets because it will keep the clock running in Paces One and Two, can be an integral play in a well-balanced offense operating in Pace Three, and it can be one of the few running plays in Paces Four and Five in order to keep the defense from simply send pass pressure every play. Therefore, it is important to evaluate each play as to where it properly fits into an offense operating at different paces. I would also generally recommend that each play sheet be colored coordinated so the play caller can easily establish which play sheet correlates with each pace. As I mentioned, paces can change quickly, so everybody involved needs to be able to adapt in a short amount of time, and if a coordinator cannot locate the proper play sheet in short order, this can delay the whole process.

When designing the play sheets, the play caller also needs to be aware of certain presnap options and the consequences of calling such plays. For example, motion, shifts, and audibles can allow valuable seconds to tick off the clock before the ball is snapped, and therefore, plays with these features should usually be located on a normal- or slow-paced play sheet. On average, presnap motion will take an additional 3 to 4 seconds, and shifts will take an additional 4 to 6 seconds, which would defeat the purpose of an offense operating in Pace Four or Five.

As discussed in the introduction, pace is defined as the speed at which an offense operates. As a result, a lot of experts measure pace by how long it takes the next play to begin after the previous play has concluded. For example, if an NFL offense is operating at a normal pace, they will generally snap the ball at an average of 31 seconds after the previous play has concluded. Meanwhile, if a team is operating in a Pace Four offense, the ball should be snapped closer to 25 seconds after the previous play. Conversely, a Pace Two NFL offense should be snapping the ball with about 3 to 5 seconds remaining on the play clock. Paces One and Five do not typically have set time frames because of a variety of factors that could affect the timing. However, in a Pace Five offense, the offense generally wants to snap the ball as soon as possible, and in a Pace One offense, the offense wants to maximize the time used on each given play, so they will want to wait until the play clock is at :01 before the ball is snapped. As a result of this, it is crucial that an offense has a visible play clock or signals indicating the time remaining. In some college and most high school stadiums, there may not be a play clock for the quarterback and offense to utilize.

When working with teams that play in these conditions, I developed a system to alert the offense of the time remaining on the play clock. For example, when an offense is in Pace One and trying to snap the ball with as little time remaining on the play clock as possible, the strategic assistant can keep track of the time on the sideline and signal to the quarterback when there is :05 remaining on the play clock, giving the QB ample time to get under center and hike the ball. I typically also advise that the co-ordinator signal to the quarterback when the play clock is at :10 so he can begin setting up and ensuring everyone is in the proper position.

In a hurry-up offense, the offensive players should be taking certain steps to preserve time as well. Once a play has concluded, the ball carrier should return the football to the referee as quickly as possible so the officials can set up for the next play. If there is a pileup, players should try their best to get out of the pile quickly and get back to the huddle or line of scrimmage. If a ball carrier is near the sideline, he should attempt to run out of bounds whenever he is able to in order to preserve additional time. If a ball carrier is unable to get out of bounds, it is also beneficial to end the play between the hash marks because it is generally a quicker play, and it will take the officials a shorter period of time to spot the ball and prepare for the next play. From a quarterback's perspective, it is more beneficial to throw the ball away if no receivers are open as opposed to taking a sack, or in some cases, even to gain a couple yards, if that requires him to stay in bounds.

If an offense is operating in Pace Four, or especially Pace Five, it may be advisable to call two plays at once, in order to reduce the time between plays. This is particularly advantageous in the last minute of a half or game when the result of the first play does not have a significant effect on the next play call, and where each second remaining on the game clock becomes more valuable. This can be accomplished with relative ease following a time-out or other clock stoppage. In these situations, the play caller should call two plays and relay them both to the quarterback in the order he would like them run. The quarterback then relays both plays to the offense in the huddle, and following the conclusion of the first play, and assuming the game clock is still running, the offense can rush to the line for the second play without having to huddle or communicate regarding the second play call. The process of calling the two plays does take some additional time, which is why it is best completed following a stoppage of the game clock. If the selection of the second play will depend on the result of the first play, a coordinator can call two secondary plays, and depending on the result of the first play, the quarterback can indicate to the offense through hand signals or verbal communication which of the secondary plays is going to be run.

Another option in the hurry-up offense is to have the quarterback wear a wristband with the plays that are on the Pace Four and Five play sheet. This can greatly assist with the signaling of plays to the quarterback and significantly reduce the amount of time it takes to pass that information along to the offense, especially at the lower levels when the quarterback may not have the benefit of a speaker in his helmet for communication purposes. It would also be beneficial in this scenario to develop a system of signals where the quarterback can communicate the play to the rest of the offense once he receives it, which would reduce the need for a huddle and preserve valuable time. When possible, teams should practice running a fast-paced offense, and most teams should incorporate a no-huddle offense and be able to operate in this fashion upon demand. A no-huddle offense can also induce fatigue on the part of the defense by preventing them from substituting or getting their correct defensive packages on the field at the appropriate times. Be aware, though, that a no-huddle offense does not necessarily mean a hurry-up offense. Again, pace is defined as the speed at which an offense is operating. Therefore, the most important factor of a Pace Four or Five offense is how much game time is used between plays, not whether a team huddles or not. For example, a team can be operating in a no-huddle offense, but not snap the ball until there are five seconds remaining on the play clock, meaning they would not be operating in a hurry-up offense.

It is also important to minimize or avoid substitutions when an offense is operating in a fast-paced offense. It takes time to get players on and off the field, which is going to use valuable seconds. Because everything is accelerated in these paces, substitutions are also more likely to cause confusion or even a penalty for illegal substitution, so limiting them will be advantageous to the offense. Additionally, plays requiring special personnel packages should be avoided for the reasons stated above. The time it will take to get the packages on and off the field will likely outweigh the benefit of any special packages.

When an offense is operating in Paces One or Two, they obviously would like to take some additional time getting to the line of scrimmage to prepare for the play. This does not necessarily require a huddle or a delay in a play call, but an offense should not line up with too much time remaining on the play clock. During these paces, a quarterback also wants to use a short snap count so he can be sure to snap the ball as close to the expiration of the play clock as necessary. Unfortunately, too many quarterbacks believe a long snap count would be beneficial here in order to utilize more time, but that can often backfire because a quarterback may start a long snap count too early for fear of a delay of game penalty and end up snapping the ball with too much time remaining on the play clock, or in the alternative, a quarterback could start the snap count too late and receive a delay of game penalty. A no-huddle offense can also be used for a slow-paced offense, and the offense can reap the benefits discussed previously, but just wait to snap the ball until the play clock is low. In this situation, the defense would have more time to rest and recover between plays since the offense is delaying snapping the ball; however, an offense can prevent defensive coordinators from substituting a new defensive package for certain plays by using a no-huddle offense.

In a slow-down offense, ideally, the ball carrier or receiver would be able to complete the play inbounds when possible. This obviously will allow the clock to continue to run, which will allow the offense to utilize more time, thereby increasing their win probability. Running plays in this pace should typically be off-tackle or sweeps as long as the player can stay inbounds, in order to use more time as well, and end-arounds are also becoming increasingly popular due to the amount of time each play takes. In a slow-down offense, quarterbacks should avoid throwing the ball away unless it is an absolute necessity. In some situations, it may be better for a quarterback to accept a sack or try to get back to the line of scrimmage and lose 1 to 3 yards in order to keep the clock running, as opposed to throwing the ball away and stopping the clock.

When the game clock is stopped between plays because of an incomplete pass, penalty, change of possession, ball carrier traveling out-of-bounds, etc., these pace principles and strategies do not apply. Under these circumstances, an offense can snap the ball as soon or as late as they would like, and the coaches have additional choices as far as presnap options and play selection. Caoches must remain cognizant of their objectives though, and be aware that their selections for the current play can have an effect on the next play, when the game clock may be running. For example, if an offense is operating in Pace Four, even if the clock is stopped between plays, a coach would not want to mass substitute players in order to run the next play, because those players would then need to be removed from the playing field following that play, and the clock may be running at that point, which will result in a loss of valuable time. In college and high school, the clock will stop when the offense earns a first down; however, this typically does not qualify as a true clock stoppage, because the game clock will restart after the chains are reset. Therefore, coaches must call the correct play and the offense must be ready to snap the ball in order to prevent the waste of too much game time.

Obviously, on fourth down plays, run/pass play selection and attempting to get out-of-bounds, or stay inbounds, may not apply. The primary goal of a fourth down play is to achieve a first down, which will ultimately be significantly more beneficial than any secondary concerns regarding the game clock. Additionally, the rules involving the stoppage of the game clock vary greatly following a fourth down play, depending on the outcome, so this should not be a large consideration of the coach unless there is very little time remaining in the game and the offense is in Pace Five.

Very few football teams properly track pace and clock management statistics. Time of possession can be, and usually is, very misleading when it comes to proper clock management principles. Remember what was discussed before, when your win probability is below 50%, your offense should generally be operating in Pace Four, meaning you may be running the same amount of plays as your opponent but have a lower time of possession because you are utilizing less time between plays. The strategic assistant should also track how often his team has one more possession than their opponent. The average is right around 50%, but by using proper clock management principles, you should be able to achieve an extra possession about 65 to 70% of the time. If a team can reach the 75% mark in this area, they are extremely successful and are greatly increasing their chances of winning those particular games.

Chapter 2 Summary

- There are generally five paces in which an offense can operate. Pace One should be selected when using as much game time as possible is your primary, and sometimes only, objective. This is commonly used late in the game when protecting a lead.

- Pace Two is when an offense is trying to score as many points as possible during a drive, but utilizing game time is a secondary goal. Offenses should generally operate in this fashion when they have a win probability of greater than 50%.

- Pace Three is the normal pace of the offense, which is used when the offense has a win probability of exactly 50%. In this situation, the sole purpose of the offense is to score as many points as possible without any concern regarding the game clock.

- When operating in Pace Four, scoring as many points as possible is a primary objective of the offense, but preserving time on the clock is a secondary goal. Offenses should be operating in this pace when their win probability is less than 50%.

- Finally, Pace Five is when the game clock is the offense's primary obstacle such as in the last minute or two of the half or game. In this pace, the primary goal is to conserve the game clock while attempting to score points as quickly as possible.

- If a greater number of plays are run in the remainder of a given game, more scoring will take place, which will result in a greater percentage chance of a lead change occurring. Therefore, if a team has a win probability greater than 50%, they would prefer to have fewer plays run throughout the rest of the game. Conversely, a team would want more plays run during the remainder of the game if they had a win probability of less than 50%. This will increase each team's chances of winning the game.

- Every team should have a goal of achieving one more effective possession than their opponents in each game. This would lead to an average increase in point production of 1.92 points, and thereby increase their odds of winning each game. In order to do this, an offense may need to operate at a pace that is inconsistent with the general pace rules, which is acceptable for this purpose.

- Each play caller should have a separate play sheet for each pace, although a specific play can appear on multiple sheets as long as it adheres to the objectives of that pace as defined above. Certain plays and presnap activities can undermine or enforce the purpose of each pace and should be only be utilized in appropriate situations as described in this chapter.

Chapter 3

TIME-OUTS

As YOU CAN imagine, no strategic or clock management book would be complete without a discussion regarding the use of time-outs. Time-outs are becoming increasingly wasted by teams and it is reducing their chances of winning particular games. Some time-outs are wasted by baseless and unwinnable challenges. Others are wasted by incorrect personnel on the field or play callers failing to communicate the play to the quarterback and other players on the field with enough time left on the play clock. So the question becomes, how do you measure the value of a time-out, and once we understand that, how do we determine when a time-out should be utilized?

If a time-out is taken immediately upon the conclusion of a play with the game clock running, as they typically should be, each time-out can preserve up to 40 seconds of game time. Based on historical calculations, an extra 40 seconds on the game clock could change the outcome in up to 4.6% of games. Assuming the average team would be benefitting from the extra 40 seconds approximately 50% of time, we can estimate that having an extra time-out, which could save the team 40 seconds when utilized correctly as we will discuss shortly, could add value in 2.3% of games for a given team. In a one-possession game in the fourth quarter, the value of a time-out can be even greater and can increase to as high as 5.8%! Obviously, having additional time-outs by eliminating wasteful uses will add to this benefit; however, it will do so at a decreasing rate.

LATE GAME TIMEOUTS

The next question then becomes, how does a team correctly use each time-out in order to maximize their win probability, which is the ultimate goal of every strategic decision? In theory, calling time-outs earlier in the half can have the same effect as calling them toward the end of the half. For example, if Team A is trailing 14–0 in the third quarter, they should be trying to preserve time by operating in Pace Four as previously discussed. Again, the reason would be that Team A would prefer more plays to be run in the remaining game time in order to provide the greatest chance to increase their win probability above 50%. Therefore, if Team A used their time-outs to preserve time in the third quarter instead of the end of the fourth quarter as is typically done, wouldn't this have the same effect on the overall game by preserving 2:00 of game time (:40 for each of their three time-outs)?

Well, the easy answer is maybe. There are two reasons why this is not normally done. First of all, the win probability could easily change before the final few minutes of the fourth quarter. If we use the example above, where Team A is trailing by 14 points in the third quarter, it is entirely possible that they could score two touchdowns, or even more, prior to the last couple minutes of the game, and therefore their win probability may now be over 50%. As a result of the change in win probability, their goal would be to reduce the time remaining on the game clock, and the time-outs they previous called would be counterproductive, and therefore would have been wasted.

Another reason why teams do not utilize their time-outs earlier than the last couple minutes of the half or game is because the opposition may not be operating in Pace One or Two. Let's break this down and discuss this further. As we covered in the last chapter, if a team has a win probability over 50%, they should be operating in Pace One or Two, depending on the situation, and not snapping the ball until just before expiration of the play clock. However, almost no teams have a strategic assistant, and therefore, many teams do not follow the correct clock management rules. As a result, many teams will actually snap the ball with 5 or 10 seconds remaining on the play clock when they have a win probability over 50%; they should be in Pace Two and may not even call the correct plays that keep the game clock moving. If the trailing team called a time-out in the third quarter to preserve time, assuming that the above statements were true, they may only be saving 25 to 30 seconds per play because the offense is not snapping the ball just before the expiration of the play clock as they should. Under this scenario, the trailing team would not be optimizing the use of their time-outs.

Conversely, if the trailing team used those same time-outs in the same situation toward the end of the fourth quarter, the offense will almost always be in Pace One trying to utilize the clock as much as possible, and a time-out at this point could save the trailing team 38 to 40 seconds. I understand that many people will say that this 10 second difference per time-out may be insignificant, but I guarantee you it is not. Remember, the purpose of clock management strategies is to leave you with one extra possession to tie or win the game, or drain the clock to prevent your opponent from having that opportunity. In many situations, 30 seconds can be the difference between one team having the last possession with an opportunity to win the game versus not having that chance. As you recall, an extra 40 seconds can potentially change the outcome of up to 4.6% of games. The purpose of clock management and these other strategies is to provide a team with every opportunity to win a particular game.

Now, the question is when should a team use their time-outs to preserve time when their win probability is below 50%? Typically, a coach should wait until he is confident that he understands what the situation will be at the end of the game before he begins utilizing any of his team's time-outs. For example, if a team is trailing by 14 points with 5 minutes left in the game, a coach can be fairly certain that his team will need to be operating in Pace Four or Five and can begin using his time-outs earlier than a team that is trailing by 3 points with the same 5 minutes left. In this second scenario, a coach would not want to use his time-outs too soon because when a team is only trailing by 3 points, a team's win probability can fluctuate very quickly. Even if that team is on defense, they can regain possession through a turnover, which may possibly increase their win probability over 50%, where they would then be in a position to use the game clock instead of conserve time. Therefore, once a coach can anticipate with reasonable certainty that his team's win probability will be below 50% as the game winds down, he can begin utilizing time-outs as long as the next requirement is satisfied as well.

Secondly, if you are using a time-out to preserve time on the clock because your win probability is below 50%, you do not want to use the time-outs until the offense is operating in Paces One or Two, and snapping the ball just prior to the expiration of the play clock. As discussed above, this will allow you to maximize the amount of time conserved by each time-out. Once these two prerequisites are met, a coach can begin using his time-outs in accordance with proper clock management principles.

A lot of coaches will delay in using their time-outs to preserve time until they are in a do-or-die set of downs. This is when the offense is operating in Pace One and one more first down will allow them to run out the clock and end the game. This is not always the best decision though. A coach may end up not needing a time-out because of an incomplete pass, penalty, or a ball carrier going out-of-bounds. As unbelievable as that may sound, it happens on a regular basis. In this situation, a coach who delayed using his time-outs may end up finishing the game with one or two time-outs remaining, or they may use them later in the game in a different scenario, without ever being able to reap the full benefit of using them properly to preserve the clock. Therefore, a coach should call them as soon as he understands when and why they are needed, and the offense is operating in Pace One, as stated previously.

A lot of people will read the last paragraph and say to themselves, "If a coach delayed using his time-outs on defense, and the offense threw an incomplete pass, he can still use the time-outs on that coach's last offense possession, so that is not a problem." While that statement is true, it is not the most effective use of a time-out. In the NFL, and this concept applies to other levels as well, the 40 second play clock begins at the conclusion of the previous play. As a result, if the offense is operating in Pace One to protect a lead, they can utilize a maximum of 40 seconds between plays. Therefore, if a defense calls a time-out at the immediate conclusion of a play where the game clock is running, they can preserve a maximum of 40 seconds of game time. However, if a team saves any of those time-outs until they are on offense so they can stop the clock between offensive plays, the time-outs can be much less effective.

On average, if an NFL offense is operating in Pace Five, they can get to the line of scrimmage and snap the ball approximately 10 to 13 seconds after the conclusion of the previous play. So, if a time-out was used on offense to stop the clock immediately after the conclusion of a play, it will save the offense only 10 to 13 seconds. Based on this calculation, you can see why it is much more beneficial for a team trailing in a game with a win probability below 50% to utilize their time-outs at the end of the game while on defense, as opposed to saving them for when they retake possession. As a result, each time-out called on defense in this situation can preserve up to 30 seconds of additional time than a time-out called on offense.

As a general rule, time-outs should only be called in the second and fourth quarters, and the reason for this is very simple. At the end of each of those quarters, there is no continuity such as after the first and third quarters, where the offense retains possession at the same yard line where they previously possessed the ball. Therefore, there is not a benefit to preserving game time prior to the expiration of these quarters. However, a team possessing the ball at the end of the second and fourth quarters will lose that possession if the game clock expires prior to the completion of their possession. Obviously, there are some exceptions to this rule. In today's game, time-outs are called in the first and third quarters very consistently, such as to avoid a delay-of-game penalty or because incorrect personnel is on the field. This may or may not be justified, and we will discuss that momentarily. However, there are acceptable circumstances in which to call a time-out in the first and third quarters. For example, wind or inclement weather can play a factor in this decision. If an offense is lining up for a field goal with a strong wind at their back with the third quarter about to expire, it may be beneficial to call a time-out to allow the offense to kick that same direction. Otherwise, if the quarter expires prior to the field goal attempt, the teams will switch directions and the offense will now be kicking into the wind.

The evaluation of this decision is rather simple. Will a made field goal increase that team's win probability more than saving a time-out? In most instances, the answer to this question will be in the affirmative, assuming a field goal in the other direction cannot be made or should not be attempted. This should be calculated by the strategic assistant and relayed to the coach so he can decide whether he should use a time-out to preserve the direction of the drive.

This is generally the same evaluation and calculation that is done when an offense is facing a penalty as discussed above. Let's assume the offense is facing first and 10, and the play clock is running down. Would it be a better decision to accept a delay-of-game penalty or use a time-out in order to maintain the current field position and distance to gain? The answer to that depends in the situation. Assuming all else is equal, accepting a 5-yard penalty, which would make it first down and 15 yards to go, would decrease your first down percentage by about 9%. In the NFL, the average offense earns a first down when facing first and 10 approximately 66% of the time. Meanwhile, an offense facing first and 15 will earn a first down about 57% of the time. The overall effect on your win probability would be less than 1%. Remember, a time-out has an average effect of 2.3% on your win percentage. Therefore, all else being equal, it may be a better option for a team to retain their time-out and accept the 5-yard penalty in the example above. However, if we examine a situation where an offense is facing a third down and 2 yards to go in the fourth quarter, accepting a 5-yard penalty could decrease the offense's win probability by almost 5%, making it wise to utilize the time-out. Again, this will depend on the constant evaluation of win probability and having the strategic assistant adequately educate the quarterback and head coach to be able to estimate these calculations when the situation requires it.

Currently, head coaches usually assume the responsibility of determining when to call time-outs to preserve time in the final several minutes of a half or game. Unfortunately, this can be an ineffective process. As we have previously discussed, the head coach will have two to four other decisions to consider at that same time, which can result in inaccurate or slow evaluations of whether to call a time-out. This will lead to time-outs being called at incorrect times, or if they are called at correct times, several valuable seconds may tick off the clock because it took the coach a short while to decide whether or not to call the time-out because of other considerations he has at that time. Remember, time-outs to conserve clock should be called immediately after the conclusion of the play, and any delay is unnecessarily decreasing a team's win probability. Although it is difficult for a head coach to relinquish such power, it is generally a much more effective process to have the strategic assistant evaluate ahead of time when certain time-outs should be called and relay this information to the head coach. This coordinator can properly evaluate the current game situation ahead of time and prepare the head coach accordingly as to whether one should be called, allowing the head coach to call it immediately following the conclusion of the play and save valuable time.

Typically, time-outs should either be called just prior to the expiration of the play clock or immediately following the conclusion of the previous play, depending on in what pace the offense is currently operating. If an offense is proceeding in Paces One or Two, again, the secondary goal is to utilize as much of the game clock is necessary, and therefore, they would want to call a time-out as close to the expiration of the play clock as possible in order to reduce the amount of time remaining on the game clock. On the other hand, if a team is currently operating in Paces Four or Five, the team's goal is to preserve game time, and as a result, would prefer to call time-outs immediately after the conclusion of the previous play in order to save game time. Again, these clock management rules would not apply or have any effect if the game clock is stopped. There are some exceptions to this rule, such as if your offense was operating in Pace Three or if you were setting up for a field goal in the final seconds of a half or game. Obviously, when setting up for a last-second field goal, the play clock can be irrelevant and the time-out should be called according to the time remaining on the game clock, which we will cover shortly.

Ideally, time-outs should only be utilized by teams to allow their offense time to run additional plays, but this is not always the case, as time-outs will be called to avoid penalties or due to incorrect player personnel, as discussed above. However, this is not the ideal use of a time-out. Think about it. An offensive team should be calling a time-out to stop the game clock in order to allow them additional time in which to operate. Conversely, a defensive team should be calling a time-out when an offense is operating in Paces One or Two so they can preserve the game clock and allow their offense time to run additional plays. Calling a time-out can allow an offense to run up to an additional seven plays, with the average pass play lasting just over 5 seconds. Therefore, assuming an offense can stop the clock after every play via an incomplete pass or the ball carrier getting out-of-bounds, the 40 seconds saved by calling a time-out while on defense can allow a corresponding offense to run up to an additional seven plays. On average, it will likely be closer to four to five plays because the offense will not always have the ability to stop the game clock following each play. Finally, a time-out should rarely be used by an offense during Paces One or Two because your goal again is to keep the game clock running, and a time-out should never be used when the game clock is stopped, as there is no added benefit whatsoever.

In the NFL, the clock management rules regarding calling time-outs are somewhat unique because of the 2-minute warning. Many coaches wonder if a defensive team trying to preserve game time for their offense on an ensuing possession should call time-outs before or after the 2-minute warning in order to properly conserve time. I have heard many analysts argue that a time-out should not be called with less than 2:40 remaining because you will be conserving less than 40 seconds due to the 2-minute warning, and therefore, not using that time-out as effectively as possible. This is not entirely correct. Let's use the following as an example to discuss this point. Assume a defense is facing a second down with 10 yards to go, with 2:45 remaining on the game clock. On second down, the offense runs a play that lasts 8 seconds, leaving 2:37 on the game clock and leaving them facing a third down. If the defense called a time-out immediately following the second down play, the third down play would begin at approximately the 2:37 mark, and no matter how long that play lasted, assuming the game clock continues to run after the play and the offense did not achieve a first down, the clock will automatically stop at the 2-minute warning, and the offense would be facing a fourth down with 2:00 remaining. However, if the defense proceeded in a different fashion as suggested by some analysts, and did not call a time-out following the conclusion of the second down play because the time-out would not preserve an entire 40 seconds, the clock would wind down to the two minute warning prior to the third down play, and assuming the next play lasted the same 5 seconds, the defense would call a time-out and be facing a fourth down with about 1:55 remaining. Therefore, as demonstrated by this example, it would generally be more beneficial to call the time-out before reaching the 2-minute warning.

Now, there is one exception to this situation. Do not ever call a time-out to preserve time on defense when less than 2:07 is remaining on the game clock, even though the basic clock management principles stated above suggest using time-outs prior to the 2-minute warning. The purpose of this exception is simple. Typically, when an offense is operating in Pace One in order to drain the clock, they can become very one-dimensional and simply run the ball every play in order to ensure the clock continues to move after each play. This can allow the defense to prepare accordingly and focus more on defending the running game, whether that means inserting run defense personnel or stacking more defenders near the line of scrimmage.

However, if a time-out is called with less than 2:07 remaining in the half or game, the offense can suddenly become two-dimensional. This is because an intelligent offensive play caller should realize that the game clock will stop following the next play due to the 2-minute warning, regardless of the outcome of the play, and therefore they can call a run or pass play. This will require the defense to modify their play call and have to defend against either option, thereby possibly exposing themselves to certain plays. As a result, I recommend never calling a defensive time-out to preserve the game clock with less than 2:07 remaining, if the 2-minute warning is upcoming. In other levels that do not have a 2-minute warning, this exception can simply be ignored as it is not applicable.

Another common mistake made by coaches is unnecessarily "saving" a time-out. Do not fall into this trap. Head coaches are constantly evaluating whether to use time-outs in the last several minutes of a close football game, and they are often faced with the decision of using a time-out now versus saving it for some future, unknown situation. Generally, if a team should use a time-out according to the principles and strategies contained in this book, then the time-out should be utilized at that moment. There is no use in saving a time-out when a coach has no idea what the circumstances will be in the future; the opportunity is present to call the time-out now, and any delay in calling the time-out could reduce its effectiveness.

LAST SECOND FIELD GOAL

If a team will need a last-second field goal to tie or win a game, a head coach should not plan on saving a time-out in order to set up the field goal unit versus utilizing it on defense prior to obtaining possession of the football. Again, as analyzed earlier, a time-out when the offense is operating in Pace One will save a defense up to 40 seconds. Meanwhile, on average, it takes an offense about 20 to 25 seconds to get the field goal unit on the field and set up to snap the ball. As a result, it would be more beneficial to use that time-out on defense to preserve 40 seconds, as opposed to saving it for the 25 seconds needed to set up the field goal unit.

It has become commonplace for defenses to call time-outs in order to "ice" a kicker prior to a final field goal attempt to tie or win a game. While it is impossible to measure the effectiveness of this technique, if a coach plans to implement this strategy, he needs to call the time-out prior to the offensive line getting set up. In discussions with kickers, if a time-out is going to be called, most prefer the time-out to be called just before the snap, so they can continue the play and execute a practice kick in order to test the field and weather conditions. This would be similar to allowing a professional golfer to have a practice putt from the exact spot of his next shot in order to better read the green. In this scenario, the kicker can generally make any necessary corrections after the "practice" kick on the following play, when the game is on the line. As a result, if a coach is planning to call a time-out, he should do so prior to the offensive line getting set up, and a defensive lineman should put his hands on the ball once the whistle is blown in order to prevent the center from snapping the ball for the practice kick.

Conversely, from an offensive standpoint, the opposite is true. If a team is lining up for a late field goal to tie or win the game and the defense may call a time-out to ice the kicker, make sure the center is lined up over the ball as early as possible so if the defense calls that time-out, the center can snap the ball and allow the kicker an opportunity for a practice kick. I have seen many instances where the offense snaps the ball 2 to 3 seconds after the time-out is called to set up the practice kick and have yet to see a penalty called by the referees. Therefore, an offense should be ready for such a situation so they can take advantage accordingly. Finally, a defense should not use a time-out to ice a kicker if the game clock is stopped with more than 12 seconds because they may be getting the ball back and could possibly use that time-out in the subsequent possession to preserve time.

If an offense is preparing for a last-second field goal in order to tie or win the game and the game clock is running, the head coach should call a time-out with 3 seconds left. A field goal will generally take between 4 to 7 seconds. If the field goal attempt begins with :03 remaining, this will allow the clock to expire on the final kick and the defense will not have a chance to return the ensuing kickoff or run another play. Additionally, if there is a bad snap or other issue, starting the play with 3 seconds remaining on the game clock should allow the offense to take a knee and call a time-out in order to set up for a second opportunity at the field goal.

If an offense does not have a time-out remaining and needs to stop the clock but the ball carrier cannot get out of bounds, some would suggest fumbling the ball out of bounds, which would subsequently stop the clock. However, this must be inadvertent as both the NFL and NCAA have a penalty for such actions that will result in a 10 second runoff for an intentional fumble out-of-bounds. Another trick that can be used by offenses in order to stop the clock between plays without utilizing a time-out is to request a measurement if the previous play is concluded near the first-down line. This will only stop the clock while the measurement is conducted, and upon completion, it will restart, so an offense should be prepared to snap the ball soon afterward. As a result of the clock restarting, this will generally not help a defense; however, it could allow them to substitute personnel if they are otherwise prevented from doing so by an offense operating in a no-huddle fashion.

Some NFL coaches have also used a challenge with a low likelihood of success because they were planning on calling a time-out anyway, which is obviously the penalty for an unsuccessful challenge. This is only acceptable if the time-out complies with the rules of clock management outlined in this book and an unsuccessful challenge will not eliminate a coach's ability to challenge a play later in the game. In the NFL, a coach is only allowed two challenges per game unless he is successful with both of them, and therefore, he should never use this technique if it is the second challenge of the game for that team, or if it is the team's first challenge but the game is still in the first half. A coach may need that challenge later in the game, which can be much more valuable than any benefit of calling the time-out.

CHAPTER 3 SUMMARY

- Time-outs can be an integral part of clock management and influence win probability, so they should not be wasted or utilized in less than optimal situations.
- Time-outs should be used as soon as the appropriate situation arises. Saving them can reduce the effect of a time-out.
- Ideally, time-outs should only be used in the second and fourth quarters and when a team is operating in Pace Four or Five.
- The purpose of an effective time-out is to allow an offense to run more plays and should usually be called immediately after the conclusion of the previous play.
- When a team is trying to preserve time, calling a time-out while on defense will be more effective and save approximately 40 seconds of game time, as opposed to calling one while on offense where it only takes 10 to 13 seconds to reset and snap the ball for the next play.
- When facing a penalty, an offense should only call a time-out to prevent a penalty if doing so will decrease their win probability less than the ensuing penalty.
- A head coach should utilize a strategic assistant or coordinator in order to evaluate when a time-out should be called in the waning moments of a game because the head coach will typically have two to four other decisions to consider at a given time, which could delay the use of a time-out and waste valuable seconds.
- It is usually more beneficial for a defense to call a time-out to preserve time prior the 2-minute warning, unless the game clock is approaching the 2-minute warning.
- When using a time-out to set up for a last-second field goal, utilize that time-out when the game clock reads :03.

Chapter 4

FOURTH DOWNS

In addition to clock management, one of the most important strategic aspects that can affect every game is the decisions that are made on fourth down. This can significantly change a team's win probability, and currently, most coaches are not following the correct decision-making process. As a result, coaches are consistently making incorrect decisions. One of the most analyzed and discussed topics in football involves a head coach's alternatives on fourth down, specifically whether to go for it, punt, or kick a field goal. As you will see shortly, coaches are often too conservative and their decisions are commonly the statistically incorrect option. This means they are making decisions that are actually hurting their team's win probability, instead of increasing it.

Just like a card player following a blackjack decision chart will give himself the best chance to win, a coach following a statistically accurate fourth down decision chart will do the same. Several reports and studies have been done on this subject, and despite similar conclusions, coaches are seemingly ignoring the results. The question I have for most coaches is, "How do you determine when to punt the ball versus attempting to convert the first down or kick a field goal?" Most coaches acknowledge that they do not have a process in place to evaluate their options on fourth down. Instead, they make the decision based on historical tendencies and gut instinct. However, how are coaches sure that these historical tendencies that have been utilized for decades are the correct choices? The unfortunate truth is that these tendencies are based on out-of-date principles and inaccurate assumptions, as we will explore in this chapter. Every coach should have a process in place to be followed on typical fourth downs in order to evaluate the best possible decision, which should be based on sound statistical data.

Before we discuss the analysis, we need to cover some basic information and definitions to ensure an understanding of the underlying principles that are relied upon in developing the fourth down decision chart. A team's first down probability is the percentage chance that a team will gain a first down in the current series, accounting for the down, yards to go, and other circumstances affecting the game. The result of this calculation is an important factor in determining the proper decision on fourth down. This calculation will also affect future play calls because the offensive play caller should be focused on putting his team in the best position to gain a first down, which in turn will extend a drive and increase a team's win probability.

For example, if an offense is facing a third down and 9 yards to go, they may have a relatively low first down percentage, in the range of 36%. But, the goal of the third down play may be to gain 6 to 8 yards to put them in a manageable position to gain a first down on fourth down, instead of trying to gain all 9 yards on third down. The 6 to 8 yards will usually be easier to gain for an offense as well because defenses are often trained to "play the sticks," meaning they are willing to allow an offense to gain some yardage as long as they do not achieve a first down.

It is also important to understand "expected value," as this concept will be utilized in this analysis as well. Again, expected value is simply the average value, or net point difference, a team would expect to experience from a given decision if they repeated the decision and process an infinite number of times and took the average result. An expected value can also be negative, which would mean that given the situation and circumstances, a team's opponent is likely to outscore them in the near future. Sometimes, a decision to be made may contain two alternatives, each with a negative expected value. In these situations, the goal would be to select the option with the lowest negative expected value in an effort to reduce the amount of points an opponent is expected to score.

Based on recent statistical data from the past 10 seasons, it appears that NFL head coaches are making an incorrect decision on fourth down approximately 19% of the time, and college coaches are doing the same on about 16.6% of such occasions. This means that, on average, coaches are making incorrect decisions on fourth down at least twice a game. The results of these incorrect decisions are ending offensive drives prematurely or not maximizing the points per drive, thereby greatly reducing a team's win probability, which again, is counterproductive to the purpose of every strategic football decision.

Historical data also suggests that the farther a team drives down the field, the more likely it is that the head coach will make an incorrect decision on fourth down. By evaluating every NFL game from 2000–2013, the incorrect choices on fourth downs are reducing a team's scoring by approximately 3.2 points per game! This means that if the correct statistical play calls were made on every fourth down, each team would increase their scoring by an average of 3.2 points per game. Think about how many games are decided each year by 3 points or less. In most cases, the losing team could have won the game by simply implementing these proper fourth down strategies. Following the concepts provided in this chapter could increase a team's chances of winning a particular game by as much as 24%! That is why this could individually be the most important chapter of this book. As we discussed in the introduction, coaches will be very reluctant to follow some of these concepts because they will be heavily criticized by people without a clear understanding of statistical analysis when they do not work out correctly. However, each coach must understand and believe that he is making the correct decision for long term success, whether or not it he is successful on a specific play.

The analysis of how a coach should proceed on fourth down is based on the expected value of each possible decision of the head coach. The expected value will factor in the likelihood of success of each decision, the probability and amount of points that will result from such a decision, and the opponent's likelihood of scoring resulting from the head coach's decision. For instance, if the coach for Team A chooses to go for it on fourth down, the statistical analysis not only identifies the likelihood of attaining a first down and the amount of points Team A can expect to score if they gain the first down based on historical data, but also includes the probability that Team A will be unsuccessful on fourth down, and the amount of points Team A can expect to surrender on the ensuing possession to Team B based on the decision made by Team A. Factoring in all this data, the expected value would then be the net amount of points Team A would expect to realize from such a decision. The expected value is then calculated for each of the other fourth down options, and the optimal choice for a team would therefore be the one with the highest expected value, or lowest negative expected value. In general, an offense's expected value will increase the farther it drives down the field. A team's expected value will be positive if they have possession of the ball and are facing a first and 10 outside of their own 15 yard line. If a team has possession inside their own 10 yard line, their expected value will actually be negative given the field position.

EXPECTED VALUE CALCULATIONS

In order calculate the expected value of choosing to go for it on fourth down, the analysis would be divided into two parts to account for whether the attempt was successful or not. If the offense is able to achieve a first down on the play, the expected value of that decision would be the amount of points the offense would expect to score based on the field position after the play. However, if the offense is unsuccessful in their attempt to gain a first down, the expected value of that decision would be equal to the expected value of the opponent based on the field position where they took possession of the football. This can be a little difficult to understand in abstract form, so I will provide an example shortly. The calculation to determine the expected value of choosing to go for it would be as follows:

$$(PG \times EVO) + [(1 - PG) \times -EVD]$$

PG equals the offense's probability of gaining a first down on the play; EVO represents the expected value of the offense if they are successful on fourth down based on their field position; and EVD equals the expected value of the defense's next possession if the offense is unsuccessful on the attempt. Now, let me use an example to illustrate this analysis. Let's assume an offense is facing a fourth down and 2 yards to go on the opponent's 45 yard line; their probability of success on fourth down would be approximately 60%, so the expected value of that decision would be as follows:

$$(0.60 \times 2.3) + [(1 - 0.6) \times -1.8] = 0.66$$

This calculation demonstrates that if the offense chose to go for it in the scenario described above, they could expect that decision to result in 0.66 points for them. The analysis also assumes that if a first down is gained, it is done by the minimum amount possible, and if the offense is unsuccessful, the defense would take over at the line of scrimmage of the previous play. Obviously, if the offense gains more yards than necessary to achieve the first down, their expected value would be even greater.

Calculating the expected value of a punt is relatively simple as well. Depending on the location of the line of scrimmage, we can estimate what the average net punt yardage will be from that specific point using NFL data since the 2000 season. The location on the field can have a significant effect on the type of punt. For instance, if the line of scrimmage is within a team's own 35 yard line, the goal of the punter will likely be to kick the ball as high and far as possible. However, that strategy will obviously change as the line of scrimmage progresses down the field, as directional and strategic punts will become more prevalent. Based on the net average punt distance, we can then estimate where the opposition will take over possession of the ball following the punt and calculate the expected value from that yard line, which would be the average amount of points scored when an offense starts first and 10 from that point. For example, an average punt in the NFL from a team's own 30 yard line will have an average net distance of 39 yards, meaning that if Team A chooses to punt from their own 30 yard line, they can expect Team B to begin their possession from their own 31 yard line. In the NFL, when a team starts first and 10 from their own 31 yard line, that team will score an average of 1 point per possession. Therefore, Team A would have an expected value of -1 if they chose to punt from their own 30 yard line.

When calculating the expected value of a field goal attempt, the result is going to be significantly related to the likelihood of a successful kick, which in turn is correlated to the distance of the kick. The expected value of a kick is outlined in the equation below:

$$[MA \times (3 - KEV)] + [(1 - MA) \times -FEV]$$

MA represents the percentage chance of a successful field goal attempt; KEV equals the expected value of the kickoff if the field goal is made (described below); and FEV is the expected value of the non-kicking team if the field goal is unsuccessful and the non-kicking team assumes possession afterward. For example, if an NFL kicker is attempting a 40-yard field goal, he would make the field goal approximately 80% of the time, but if the kick was unsuccessful, the opposing team would have an expected value of 0.9 points factoring in the chance of a blocked field goal. As a result, this field goal attempt would have an expected value as calculated below:

$$[0.80 \times (3 - 0.7)] + [(1 - 0.80) \times -0.9)] = 1.14$$

So the kicking team would have an expected value of 1.14 points if they chose to kick a field goal in this situation.

In calculating the expected value of a kickoff, the average starting field position after a kickoff in the NFL is just past the receiving team's 22 yard line since the kickoff was moved up to the 35 yard line following the 2011 season. When a team begins a drive at their own 22 yard line, their expected value is 0.7 points. This is significant because almost every score precedes a subsequent kickoff, and to calculate the true value of a coaching decision, if that decision results in a score, you must also take into effect the expected value of the ensuing possession. Therefore, if one is calculating the expected value of attempting a field goal, the expected value of a made field goal is not 3 points, but instead 2.3 points due to the ensuing kickoff, unless that field goal is made upon completion of the half or game. Again, you must subtract the expected value of the subsequent kickoff (0.7) from the actual points scored.

Now, let's put this all together to evaluate how to properly conduct the analysis for all three fourth down options. Let's assume Team A is facing a fourth down and 2 yards to go from the opponent's 40 yard line. From this field position, the average net punt distance is 27 yards, which would mean that Team B would take possession at their own 13 yard line, where they would have an expected value of 0, which would then become the total expected value of this option. To calculate the expected value of attempting a field goal in the situation described above, we would use the equation from earlier:

$$[0.41 \times (3 - 0.7)] + [(1 - 0.41) \times -1.8)] = -0.12 \text{ points}$$

Therefore, a field goal would have an expected value of -0.12 points, so it would be a worse option than punting, which has an expected value of 0. Finally, we would calculate the expected value of going for it on fourth down, as follows:

$$(0.49 \times 2.8) + [(1 - 0.49) \times -1.4] = 0.658 \text{ points}$$

So what does this data mean? Well, a coach would typically compare the results from each of the three options and select the one with the highest expected value because this would predict that on average, that would result in the highest net difference of points for his team. As a result of this analysis, we know that punting would have an expected value of 0 points, meaning this option would be completely neutral and not benefit either team. Meanwhile, kicking a field goal would have an expected value of -0.12 points, which would demonstrate that if a coach selected this option, the opponent would outscore his team by an average of 0.12 points based on this decision. Finally, if a coach chose to go for it in this situation, his team would have an expected value of 0.658, indicating that his team would outscore the opponent by an average of 0.658 points based on this selection. The ultimate goal is to always select the option with the highest expected value, which would offer the greatest benefit to that team. Therefore, going for it would be the best option under these circumstances.

Even though these numbers seem small, bear in mind how many fourth downs a team faces in a typical game, and making the correct decision could end up being a 7 to 10 point swing, which could ultimately determine the outcome of many games. This same analysis can be performed on every fourth down in order to determine the most beneficial option. An abbreviated copy of the fourth down decision chart can be found on an upcoming page. As you will see from the chart, there are many instances when a coach should go for it on fourth down, including any time there are 3 yards or less to gain for the first down, regardless of field position. I understand this is a far cry from the decisions that coaches currently make during games. However, again, statistically these are the correct decisions, and this chart should be followed in order to provide a team with the best opportunity to win. Obviously, it is not going to work in a coach's favor every time he chooses to go for it, but coaches must remember that over time, the benefits of these decisions will outweigh any detriments.

Because coaches following this chart will have significantly more fourth down attempts than they usually face, it would be wise for them to incorporate several additional plays into their playbook to achieve a 3 to 5 yard gain to be used on fourth down, as well as possible 2-point conversion plays. Because a team will likely have 3 to 5 additional fourth downs in which they attempt to convert, it is important to ensure you have enough plays to cover such situations. A copy of the fourth down decision chart can be found on the following page:

FOURTH DOWN DECISION CHART

Yard Line	Yards to Go											
	1	2	3	4	5	6	7	8	9	10	11	12
Own 5	Go For It	Go For It	Punt	Punt	Punt	Punt	Punt	Punt	Punt	Punt	Punt	Punt
Own 10	Go For It	Go For It	Go For It	Punt	Punt	Punt	Punt	Punt	Punt	Punt	Punt	Punt
Own 15	Go For It	Go For It	Go For It	Punt	Punt	Punt	Punt	Punt	Punt	Punt	Punt	Punt
Own 20	Go For It	Go For It	Go For It	Punt	Punt	Punt	Punt	Punt	Punt	Punt	Punt	Punt
Own 25	Go For It	Go For It	Go For It	Go For It	Punt	Punt	Punt	Punt	Punt	Punt	Punt	Punt
Own 30	Go For It	Go For It	Go For It	Go For It	Punt	Punt	Punt	Punt	Punt	Punt	Punt	Punt
Own 35	Go For It	Go For It	Go For It	Go For It	Punt	Punt	Punt	Punt	Punt	Punt	Punt	Punt
Own 40	Go For It	Go For It	Go For It	Go For It	Punt	Punt	Punt	Punt	Punt	Punt	Punt	Punt
Own 45	Go For It	Go For It	Go For It	Go For It	Go For It	Punt	Punt	Punt	Punt	Punt	Punt	Punt
50	Go For It	Go For It	Go For It	Go For It	Go For It	Punt	Punt	Punt	Punt	Punt	Punt	Punt
Opp 45	Go For It	Go For It	Go For It	Go For It	Go For It	Go For It	Punt	Punt	Punt	Punt	Punt	Punt
Opp 40	Go For It	Go For It	Go For It	Go For It	Go For It	Go For It	Go For It	Field Goal	Field Goal	Field Goal	Field Goal	Field Goal
Opp 35	Go For It	Go For It	Go For It	Go For It	Go For It	Go For It	Go For It	Go For It	Field Goal	Field Goal	Field Goal	Field Goal
Opp 30	Go For It	Go For It	Go For It	Go For It	Go For It	Go For It	Field Goal	Field Goal	Field Goal	Field Goal	Field Goal	Field Goal
Opp 25	Go For It	Go For It	Go For It	Go For It	Field Goal	Field Goal	Field Goal	Field Goal	Field Goal	Field Goal	Field Goal	Field Goal
Opp 20	Go For It	Go For It	Go For It	Go For It	Field Goal	Field Goal	Field Goal	Field Goal	Field Goal	Field Goal	Field Goal	Field Goal
Opp 15	Go For It	Go For It	Go For It	Go For It	Field Goal	Field Goal	Field Goal	Field Goal	Field Goal	Field Goal	Field Goal	Field Goal
Opp 10	Go For It	Go For It	Go For It	Go For It	Field Goal	Field Goal	Field Goal	Field Goal	Field Goal	Field Goal	Field Goal	Field Goal
Opp 5	Go For It	Go For It	Go For It	Field Goal	Field Goal	x	x	x	x	x	x	x

Table 4.1

Obviously, the fourth down calculation is an average and can vary greatly from that figure. An opponent will not always begin their possession at their own 22 yard line following a kickoff; however, because that is the average, we use that yard line in our expected value calculations. For example, after a safety, the average starting field position following the free kick is the receiving team's 38 yard line, which equates to an expected value of 1.3 points for that possession. Therefore, the expected value of a safety is actually 3.3 points (2 points + 1.3 points).

The goal of the expected value calculations is to evaluate which option would result in the highest net scoring difference because it is based on the premise that in order to have the greatest chance of winning a particular game, a team should aim to score as many points as possible and limit the amount of points their opponent will score. These calculations are similar to those used in baseball, where statistical analysts determine the value of a player by estimating the amount of runs that player will contribute to the offense and how many runs he will prevent on defense. These calculations are utilized to increase the amount of net points a team will score.

However, sometimes scoring the maximum amount of points is not what will give a team the optimum chance of winning a particular game. For example, let's assume a team is trailing by 2 points and facing fourth down and goal from the opponent's 2 yard line with 30 seconds left in the game. In this case, the offense's goal would not be to score as many points as possible, but rather to make sure they accumulate enough points to take the lead. As a result, even though the above analysis would demonstrate that going for it would have the greatest expected value for the offense, it would be the correct decision to stray from the formula and kick the field goal in order to take the lead. This would provide the offense with the highest win probability as opposed to trying for the touchdown because of the limited time left in the game. This example proves that not all points are equal, and the above equations are to be used when game appropriate. Again, in determining what course of action to select on fourth down, a coach should understand that the sole purpose of the fourth down decision chart below is to maximize net scoring in order to increase a team's win probability, but it does not factor in game situation or time remaining.

Additionally, a coach may need to expand the fourth down decision chart in the last 5 minutes or so of the game if his team is trailing. He may need to become more aggressive with his offensive decision making because of the possibility his team may not obtain possession of the ball again if they punt it. A coach must balance the possibility of getting a stop on the next defensive possession and scoring versus the chance of a successful fourth down play. In order to do this, expected value and win probability must both be factored into account in order for the coach to make the optimal decision.

Another aspect that can alter the expected value formula is the strength and skill level of a kicker. In general, NFL kickers are more accurate than NCAA kickers, and this idea continues down to the lower levels as well. As a result, NFL kickers will have a greater probability of converting a field goal from a given spot, which will increase the expected value of kicking such a field goal from any field position. Consequently, a coach may need to reevaluate and customize the fourth down decision chart included in this chapter because it was based on NFL kicking averages. Even at the same level of football, not all kickers are created equal, and therefore, even NFL teams cannot use the exact same chart, because some kickers have a stronger leg, while others may be more accurate from closer range. So a team should be sure to adjust the chart based on their kicker's ability and strengths.

After all of this analysis of the fourth down decisions, the question then becomes, why are coaches constantly making incorrect decisions on fourth downs? As mentioned previously, NFL coaches are making decisions on fourth down that differ from the statistically correct decision approximately 19% of the time, with college coaches doing so around 16.6%

of the time. With the average team facing 9 to 10 fourth downs per game, this means that a coach is making the incorrect decision about twice a game. According to the book *The Hidden Game of Football*, the two most common explanations for why coaches are making so many incorrect decisions is because coaches are often choosing to kick or punt instead of going for it because that is the historical thinking in football. Back when offenses were much less prolific, coaches were more concerned about field position and less concerned about maximizing net scoring.

In the early days of football, scoring drives were much less rare and usually resulted from long drives of 15 plays or more. Most teams would only have one or two scoring drives per game, so punting the ball and forcing the opposing team to drive 80 to 90 yards was understood to be the best decision. However, this is obviously not the case anymore. Long plays and prolific offenses are seen everywhere nowadays, with even high school teams running spread offenses. Even "defensive teams" should be following this analysis and subsequent calculations because it will still provide the best opportunity to win. Also, these statistics were not available many years ago to demonstrate to coaches what the best options would be on fourth down. However, with advanced statistical analysis and the increasing offensive numbers that are being put up on a weekly basis, coaches and teams must adapt and begin making the proper decisions. This chart is designed to be a starting point for coaches to provide the basic information necessary to properly evaluate fourth downs.

In a paper written by David Romer entitled "Do Firms Maximize," he suggests that coaches are continuing to make improper decisions on fourth down due to concerns they have over job security. He states that if coaches follow conventional wisdom and continue to be conservative on fourth down, they could avoid blame if their decisions do not work out. Alternatively, if coaches try to implement the strategies in this book and follow the recommended analysis, they would constantly be second-guessed by uninformed "football people" if their decisions were unsuccessful. For example, let's analyze a decision made by Bill Belichick of the New England Patriots in 2009. The Patriots had possession of the ball and were leading the Indianapolis Colts by 6 points with 2:08 remaining in the game. They were facing a fourth down with 2 yards to go on their own 28 yard line. Belichick made the decision to go for it but was unsuccessful, and the Colts took over possession around the Patriots 29 yard line. Soon after, the Colts scored a touchdown and ultimately won the game, and Belichick was blamed afterward for causing the Patriots' loss because of his fourth down decision. However, there was one problem... it was the correct call according to the calculations outlined above. Yes, it did not work out on this occasion, but that does not mean it was the wrong decision given the situation.

The decision by Belichick was greatly criticized by the media after the game, including former players Rodney Harrison and Trent Dilfer. Harrison called it the worst coaching decision Belichick has ever made, and Dilfer said the decision was absolutely ridiculous. This is just an example of the historical and incorrect thinking of some football players and other personnel. However, if the Patriots would have punted and the Colts scored anyway, the Patriots defense would have received the blame, even though it was the incorrect decision. Again, this shows that coaches can avoid blame by making certain fourth down decisions, even if they are incorrect and put their team in a worse position to win the game. Belichick handled the situation correctly and stood by his decision because he knew it was statistically the correct one to make, and that is the mentality coaches need to have when implementing these strategies.

Fourth Down Correlation

There are also a few final thoughts that indirectly relate to fourth downs. According to a study performed by Dr. Cade Massey, an assistant professor at Yale University, the result of first down plays is a strong indication of which team will win a given game. Massey states that a team's ability to meet certain benchmarks on each down is the best predictor of whether a drive will be successful. Massey further explains that first down can singularly be the most important down on most drives, and if an offense can gain a minimum of 4 yards on first and 10, that team is significantly more likely to achieve a first down and keep the drive alive. As a result, teams need to be more careful in their selection of first down plays, as a simple inside run that results in 2 to 3 yards or an incomplete pass when a team is attempting to "go long" can have a significant negative impact on a team's ability to attain a first down.

Teams should not construe this analysis as suggesting that a team should choose plays with a low chance of losing yards in the hope of gaining 4 yards. Instead, an offense would benefit more from plays with a certain expected gain rather than a low variance, such as short, quick passes, runs off tackle, screen passes, and so on. In order to evaluate a team's success in achieving this goal, they should be evaluating their average gain on first down per game, without including kneel-downs, first and goal situations, or drives significantly affected by the game clock, because during those situations, this analysis may be of secondary importance.

CHAPTER 4 SUMMARY

- Current coaches are making incorrect decisions on fourth down approximately 17 to 19% of the time due to outdated information and fear of the unknown.
- The analysis of how to proceed on fourth down is a function of expected value, which is the average value you would expect to experience from a given decision if you repeated the process an infinite number of times and took the average result.
- In order to determine the best option on fourth down, a coach should calculate the expected value of each option with the highest value being the optimal decision.
- The fourth down decision chart does not take into account weather conditions or time remaining in the half/game, so it may be necessary to stray from the recommended decision if the game situation dictates it.
- A coach may need to be more aggressive in the final minutes of a game in which they are trailing, and try for a first down even when the decision chart recommends a punt or field goal.
- The chart may need to be customized based on a team's individual kicker and his leg strength and accuracy.
- The average gain on first down can be a good indicator of whether a drive will be successful. Teams should generally aim to gain a minimum of 4 yards on first down.

Chapter 5

LATE-GAME AND
SPECIALTY PLAYS

THIS CHAPTER IS designed as a "catchall" to cover many different late game and specialty plays that can occur during the course of a season. The purpose of this chapter is to provide coaches with adequate information so they can make appropriate decisions and understand the recommended situations to utilize certain plays based on statistical analysis. Some of the situations to use the plays may not occur very often, but it is important to understand the statistics behind the analysis so coaches and their teams are prepared when the situation arises. Too often in today's game, coaches are calling improper late-game plays, which are reducing their win probability, and although they do not happen very often, they can be the difference between winning and losing a particular game. Because a lot of the concepts discussed in this chapter will only be implemented in a small percentage of games, it is important that the strategic assistant and coaches are familiar with these principles so they can utilize them when necessary.

An important reference point with which to begin is illustrated in the following table. Coaches will need to become familiar with this information because it will assist with certain late-game decisions and situations.

This chart lays out the minimum amount of time needed to complete a full series of downs, which is dependent on the number of time-outs a team has:

TIME-OUTS	MINIMUM GAME TIME NEEDED
0	42 seconds
1	34 seconds
2	26 seconds
3	19 seconds

Obviously, the information contained in this table is based on averages, and the game time required to run these plays will vary based on the offense's ability to get out-of-bounds and whether the game clock stops after any of the plays, such as for an incomplete pass, penalty, etc. If there is more time remaining on the game clock than indicated above, a coach needs to be cognizant of the clock and ensure the offense does not score too early and leave time for the opposing team to respond with a corresponding scoring drive. This can be accomplished by proper play calls and snapping the ball at the appropriate times as will be discussed shortly.

LATE FIELD GOALS

If an offense is attempting to drive for a late score to tie or win the game, they should use the pace graph that we previously covered in Chapter 2. If a team will be attempting a field goal on their final drive, it is important to estimate the range and accuracy of the team's kicker in order to determine how much yardage the offense must gain to put the kicker within his kicking range. In the NFL, kickers have greatly improved over the last 20 to 25 years, and most kickers can regularly succeed on a 50+ yard field goal attempt. Therefore, NFL offenses many times simply need to gain the 35 to 40 yard line so they could provide their kicker with a reasonable field goal attempt. In desperate situations without adverse weather, many kickers can regularly kick field goals from even 60 yards if necessary.

In college, most kickers experience a significant decrease in accuracy around 45 yards, so most teams would like to make it to at least the 30 yard line. High school and lower levels typically have a larger variance in the talents of each kicker, but usually snapping the ball from the 15 to 20 yard line should be within the range of most kickers. Often, head coaches can ask the kickers what they feel is their maximum distance on that day given the weather and field conditions. A kicker should be able to accurately and honestly respond to this question given the practice he was able to complete before the game or at the half. Kickers may also prefer to kick from certain field locations, such as a certain hash mark or the middle of the field, so it is important for a coach to discuss this with the kicker ahead of time and understand what benefit that will provide. In some situations, coaches may be able to set up the kicker in his preferred location and hopefully increase the chance of a successful kick.

If an offense does have a time-out remaining and the coach feels they are within field goal range, he should call a time-out with 3 to 4 seconds remaining as previously discussed. This will allow the clock to expire during the kick and not require the team to kick off afterward. If you do not believe avoiding the kickoff is particularly beneficial, refer back to the Music City Miracle. If the Buffalo Bills could have avoided the ensuing kickoff after a successful field goal attempt, they would have won that game and advanced to the second round of the playoffs. Although it does not happen often, returning a kickoff for a touchdown, or at least far enough to place the offense in field goal range, does happen. Therefore, a team should avoid having to kick off following a late score to take the lead as often as possible.

In Super Bowl XXXVI, between the St. Louis Rams and New England Patriots, this could have become an issue. In that game, the score was tied and New England had possession of the ball with less than 1 minute remaining. The Patriots drove down the field, and without any time-outs, Tom Brady spiked the ball with :07 remaining on the game clock to set up for the game-winning field goal. This was done with too much time remaining as discussed above. As a result, the kick sailed through the uprights with 2-3 seconds still remaining on the clock. In this situation, it did not matter because everyone stormed the field and the referee did not put additional time on the clock like he should have; however, the Patriots should have been forced to kick off with at least 1 second left on the clock. Brady should have spiked the ball with 3 to 4 seconds left as described above in order to avoid this issue.

If a team has possession of the ball and is trying to drive for a game-winning or game-tying field goal without a time-out, they should try to end the second-to-last play with at least 14 seconds remaining. Assuming it will take the officials approximately 10 seconds to reset the ball, this would allow the offense about 3 to 4 seconds to snap the ball and either spike the ball or attempt a field goal on the final play if it is fourth down. On these types of drives, if the offense does not have a time-out, it is recommended that they save a down to spike the ball, which would stop the clock and allow the field goal unit adequate time to prepare for the kick. It is much easier for the field goal unit to get setup and snap the ball when they do not have to worry about the game clock expiring.

In order to prepare for such situations, coaches must practice getting the field goal unit on the field and set up as quickly as possible. Head coaches should know exactly how long it takes this unit to snap the ball for the field goal attempt from the conclusion of the previous play. If the game clock is running while an offense is lining up for a final field goal, the holder should have his eye on the clock and call for the snap when the game clock hits :04 if he has that option. This will allow a few extra seconds in case the long-snapper requires them, and no one will need to panic that the clock will expire prior to the snap.

If a coach is planning to attempt a final field goal to tie or win the game, and the offense gains the necessary yardage to kick that field goal with time still remaining on the game clock, the offense should continue operating in order to hopefully gain additional yards and increase the chances of successfully converting the field goal. I understand this is an obvious concept, but I cannot tell you how many times a team reached field goal range and suddenly became conservative in their play calls to settle for a 40 to 50 yard field goal, only to watch their kicker miss the kick. In the NFL, a kicker only has about a 74% chance of making a kick within this range and even less at the younger levels.

An example of this occurred when the Chicago Bears played the Minnesota Vikings on December 1, 2013. In that game, the Bears had possession in overtime and drove down to the Vikings 32 yard line where they earned a first down. Instead of continuing to run their normal offense, they called a basic run up the middle on first down for a short gain, and on second down, they settled for a 47-yard field goal attempt for Robbie Gould, who was one of the NFL's most accurate kickers at the time. However, he pushed the kick wide right, and Minnesota drove down for the game-ending field goal. This situation happens more than it should, and this can often be the result. There was plenty of time remaining and it was only second down, so there was no reason to settle for that attempt. The Bears should have continued running their offense until they reached a fourth down or gained enough yardage to significantly increase their chances to convert a successful field goal. If the Bears offense had gained even 5 more yards, this would have increased the chance of a successful field goal by about 6%, and gaining 10 yards would have increased the probability of making the kick by almost 12%! This proved to be a costly decision as the Bears ended up missing the playoffs by a half-game that season, which shows you just how important every late-game decision can be.

In order to have a touchdown probability of at least 50%, which is the percentage chance that a team will score a touchdown on that specific possession, an offense would need to get a first down inside the opponent's 15 yard line. Therefore, if a team is trailing late in a game and needs a touchdown to win or tie the game, their goal should be to get within the opponent's 15 yard line with enough time remaining to run four additional plays. That will ensure the offense's win probability is at least 50%, which will then make them the favorite to win the game.

HAIL MARY PLAY

In football circles, a Hail Mary pass is defined as a long forward pass into the end zone late in a game or half, with little chance for success. Typically, a Hail Mary can take anywhere from 5 to 9 seconds depending on the distance the pass must travel and the time it takes the quarterback to release the ball after it is snapped. On average, when a Hail Mary pass must travel at least 40 yards in the air in order to reach the end zone, the offense will have a success rate between 2 to 4%, provided that the quarterback has a strong enough arm so that the ball will travel in the air and reach the end zone. The following chart shows the percentage chance of a successful Hail Mary pass based on the yardage to the end zone from the current line of scrimmage, calculated from information gathered since the 1996 NFL season:

DISTANCE TO GOAL LINE	CHANCE OF SUCCESS
40+ Yards	3.4%
30 to 40 Yards	5.3%
20 to 30 Yards	12.7%
10 to 20 Yards	28.4%
0 to 10 Yards	44.2%

If an offense is within Hail Mary range, meaning the quarterback can at least throw the football from the line of scrimmage to the end zone on a fly, but still outside the opponent's 30 yard line, and there are more than 9 seconds left with the offense needing a touchdown, it will statistically be more beneficial to attempt two Hail Mary passes as opposed to running a shorter play to gain yardage and then attempt a Hail Mary on the final play, unless that shorter play will get the offense within the 30 yard line, which will significantly increase the chance of completing the pass. I understand this is a lot of information to digest, but it is important that coaches understand this concept. Essentially, if a team is going to need a Hail Mary, an offense should try to drive at least to their opponent's 30 yard line, which would greatly increase the chance of a successful Hail Mary. Otherwise, if a team cannot gain the 30 yard line, they should attempt two Hail Mary passes if there is adequate time available on the game clock.

Based on the previous chart, if an offense can get within 30 yards of the end zone for the final play, they will have at least a 12.7% chance of completing a Hail Mary pass for a touchdown. However, if the line of scrimmage is outside the opponent's 30 yard line and they have time to attempt two Hail Mary passes, a team will have a 5.8% chance of completing one of the two passes for a touchdown, factoring in the chance of an interception on the first play. Therefore, two attempted Hail Mary passes would increase a team's chance of success; however, not as much as attempting the same pass from within the 30 yard line.

Additionally, a team will have a greater chance of completing a Hail Mary pass if it is not the final play of the game. When the defense is expecting such a play, they are able make player substitutions to assist with defending the play, such as utilizing taller players on defense and positioning their players appropriately where they may have 4 to 6 players positioned at or near the goal line, thereby making the pass harder to complete for the offense. However, if an offense has the opportunity to run a

Hail Mary prior to the final play of the half or game, specifically when the game clock has between 10 and 19 seconds remaining, the offense's chances of success will almost triple when outside of the 40 yard line and will more than double when the line of scrimmage is between 30 to 40 yards from the end zone. It is important to understand when the Hail Mary pass should be called in order to maximize a team's chances of success, and the strategic assistant should be able to calculate the chances of success after each play to determine the appropriate time to run such a play.

A lot of opinions have been expressed about how to defend the Hail Mary pass. If a defense is expecting this play to be run by the offense, they should place at least two taller, athletic players at or near the goal line on either side of the field to help defend the pass, even if they do not typically play defense. Most analysts and experts nowadays will simply tell defenders to knock the ball down instead of trying to intercept it. While this may be good advice in some situations, many teams are now sending trailing receivers down the field a few yards behind the play in order to catch a ball that is tapped backward by defenders attempting to knock it down. As a result of offenses adapting to this strategy, the best method to defend a Hail Mary is to have your defenders tip the ball toward the sideline or back of the end zone if they are within a couple yards of either. If the defense can force the ball to travel out of bounds, this will prevent another receiver from potentially catching a tipped ball.

LATERAL PLAYS

Like a Hail Mary pass, a "hook-and-ladder," or other lateral play, has a much lower success rate when the defense is expecting such a play. This type of play is usually run as the last play of the game when the offense needs to score but the line of scrimmage is located outside of Hail Mary range. Unlike the Hail Mary play, the hook-and-ladder or other lateral play can be run earlier in the game when the defense is not expecting it because it generally is less risky than the Hail Mary. Many coaches I have spoken with have commented that the lateral portion of the play is too risky to run when it is not necessary, and thus, they will not call the play unless it is necessary. But is the lateral any more dangerous than pitching the ball to the running back on an option play or outside sweep? Statistically, it is not, and coaches should not be afraid to call this play in certain situations earlier in the game, even when it is not necessary.

It is always a good idea for every team to have the hook-and-ladder in the playbook for desperation purposes, such as when Boise State used it to tie the game against Oklahoma in the 2007 Fiesta Bowl. However, a coach can significantly increase the chances of success using this play by calling it earlier in the game. I have seen very few statistics on the success rate of this play, other than it is 4 to 5 times more likely to result in a significant gain (more than 20 yards) when it is not called within the last minute of the game.

In some instances, a coach will have no choice but to attempt the lateral play in order to score as time is winding down. The lateral plays that are successful typically involve a cross-field pass in order to keep the proper spacing, such as the Music City Miracle that the Tennessee Titans successfully ran in the 2000 Wildcard game against the Buffalo Bills. During that play, the Titan's Frank Wycheck was handed the ball and proceeded to throw a lateral across the field to Kevin Dyson that traveled approximately 25 yards in the air. Because of the distance the ball traveled, the Bills could not recover defensively and Dyson completed the play with a 75-yard touchdown run.

In these situations where the offense will attempt a lateral play, the offensive players will want to maintain spacing and utilize clean passes or laterals of at least 5 yards. The problem with most of these plays is that every offensive player runs toward the ball, which creates a cluster that becomes easy to defend. Additionally, the non-skill offensive players, such as the lineman, must continue blocking and creating space for the skilled ball handlers. It is generally intelligent for every team to have at least two designed lateral plays in their playbook, one when they are receiving a kickoff, which usually ends up being a squib kick, and another for last-second desperation plays from a line of scrimmage where the offense needs a touchdown. Both should include proper spacing and at least one long lateral as discussed before. These plays should only be run when trailing because of the possibility of a fumble, unlike the less risky hook-and-ladder as discussed previously, which uses a much shorter lateral and thereby reduces the risk of a fumble.

When a team is leading in the final minute of the game and their opponent has possession of the ball outside of Hail Mary range, the defense must be ready for the lateral play. In this situation, it is important to spread out the defenders and make sure they remain in their lanes. The key is not to run to the ball carrier upon a reception or receipt of a lateral, but instead to maintain proper defensive spacing and be ready for a long lateral as suggested in the last paragraph. If the defense does obtain possession via a fumble or interception, that player should take a knee or run out of bounds immediately. This will prevent the offense from having an opportunity to regain possession through a turnover or have a penalty called on the defense.

Taking a Knee

Kneel-down time is the period toward the end of the game when the offense is winning and can utilize all of the time remaining on the game clock by taking a knee on each of the remaining plays, taking into account the down, amount of time remaining, location on the field, and the number of time-outs the defense has left. This is also referred to as the "victory point," because there should be no reason that the offense cannot earn the victory once they reach that point of the game.

If an offense is just outside of kneel-down time, they can use additional time by running a quarterback sweep, which would hopefully use enough time to get the offense into kneel-down time. During the quarterback sweep, the offense will overload the offensive line and wide receivers to one side, generally the side of the field with greater yardage from the spot of the football to the sideline. The quarterback will then take the snap and run toward the sideline behind the strong side of the formation, angling slightly toward his own end zone. He must be sure to slide inbounds before the defense is able to hit him in order to keep the clock running, which is the purpose of such a play. Generally, taking a knee will only utilize about 1 to 2 seconds of the game clock; however, the quarterback sweep can use up to 8 seconds. This is why it can be useful to drain additional time off the clock when an offense is just outside of kneel-down time. An offense can use an extra 20 to 25 seconds of game time on average by running four quarterback side sweeps instead of taking a knee on the same four plays. An offense will usually lose between 8 to 12 yards on every quarterback sweep, so it is also important to consider field position when running this play to ensure an offense does not bury itself too deep in its own territory when there is still time remaining on the game clock.

The tables below will outline the maximum amount of time that can be used by an offense in kneel-down time and quarterback side sweep time for each level: high school, college, and NFL. Each chart is a little different because high schools typically have a unique play clock compared to the other levels, and the NFL is the only level with a 2-minute warning. These charts take into account how many time-outs the defense has remaining and states the maximum amount of game time that can be utilized simply by using these plays and allowing the play clock to run the maximum amount following each play. Finally, these charts assume that each kneel-down play uses 1 second of game time, side-sweep plays use 7 seconds, and the reset time is 6 seconds.

HIGH SCHOOL KNEEL-DOWN TABLE				
	Defensive Time-outs Remaining			
Down	3	2	1	0
1	:04	:35	1:06	1:37
2	:03	:03	:34	1:05
3	:02	:02	:02	:33
4	:01	:01	:01	:01

COLLEGE KNEEL-DOWN TABLE				
	Defensive Time-outs Remaining			
Down	3	2	1	0
1	:04	:44	1:24	2:04
2	:03	:03	:43	1:23
3	:02	:02	:02	:42
4	:01	:01	:01	:01

NFL KNEEL-DOWN TABLE				
	Defensive Time-outs Remaining			
Down	3	2	1	0
1	:04	:44	1:24	2:00
2	:03	:03	:43	1:23
3	:02	:02	:02	:42
4	:01	:01	:01	:01

Again, these tables state the maximum amount of game time an offense can utilize by calling only kneel-down plays. For example, if the defense has two time-outs remaining and the offense was facing a first down, the offense could use a maximum of 44 seconds of game time in the NFL. Let me demonstrate where this number came from. Under this scenario, the offense would snap the ball on first down with 44 seconds remaining, and again assuming the knee play takes 1 second, the first down play would be completed with 43 seconds left, upon which the defense would call a time-out. On second down, the ball would be snapped with the same 43 seconds remaining, use one second with the kneel-down play, and the defense should call their final time-out with 42 seconds remaining. The ball would be snapped with 42 seconds remaining on third down, and since the defense would have no time-outs remaining, the 40 second play clock would wind down, and would be set to expire with 1 second left on the game clock. The offense should then snap the ball on fourth down with that 1 second remaining, and the clock would expire while that play is in progress. This same formula or sequence of events can be used for each situation detailed above. Because of the 2-minute warning in the NFL, an offense cannot utilize more than 2:00 of game time because the clock will be stopping at or around the 2:00 mark.

The QB sweep tables below contain the same data and concepts illustrated in the kneel-down tables, they just also factor in the additional time it takes to run the actual sweep play:

HIGH SCHOOL QB SWEEP TABLE				
	Defensive Time-outs Remaining			
Down	3	2	1	0
1	:28	:59	1:30	2:01
2	:21	:21	:52	1:23
3	:14	:14	:14	:45
4	:07	:07	:07	:07

COLLEGE QB SWEEP TABLE				
	Defensive Time-outs Remaining			
Down	3	2	1	0
1	:28	1:08	1:48	2:28
2	:21	:21	1:01	1:41
3	:14	:14	:14	:54
4	:07	:07	:07	:07

NFL QB SWEEP TABLE				
	Defensive Time-outs Remaining			
Down	3	2	1	0
1	:28	1:08	1:48	2:00
2	:21	:21	1:01	1:41
3	:14	:14	:14	:54
4	:07	:07	:07	:07

Similar to the example above, if the defense has two time-outs remaining and the offense was facing a first down, the offense could use a maximum of 1:08 of game time in the NFL. In this situation, the offense would snap the ball on first down with 1:08 remaining, and again, assuming the quarterback sweep play takes 7 seconds, the first down play would be completed with 1:01 remaining, which is when the defense would call a time-out. On second down, the ball would be snapped with 1:01 remaining, the offense would use 7 seconds with the sweep play, and the defense would use their last time-out with 54 seconds remaining. The ball would then be snapped with 54 seconds remaining on third down, the play would be completed with 47 seconds left, and since the defense would have no time-outs remaining, the 40 second play clock would wind down, and would be set to expire with 7 seconds left on the game clock. The offense should then snap the ball with 7 seconds remaining just before the expiration of the play clock, and the game clock should then expire as the fourth down play is completed.

From the offense's perspective, it is also important to be sure nothing is done that would result in a clock stoppage, such as an offensive penalty. Any stoppage of the clock can alter the information provided in the tables and allow more time for the defense. A recent example occurred on

October 26, 2014 in a game between the Atlanta Falcons and Detroit Lions. Atlanta was leading 21–19 and had possession of the ball at the 2-minute warning of the fourth quarter. They were facing a first down with 10 yards to go, although Detroit did have one time-out, so the Falcons were slightly outside of kneel-down time. However, the Falcons should have been operating in Pace One with the ultimate goal of using up the game clock.

The Falcons ran the ball up the middle for a gain of 1 yard on first down, and the Lions called their last time-out with 1:58 remaining. The Falcons made their first mistake by not calling a run play that would use more than 2 seconds of the game clock. At this point, even if the Falcons simply took a knee on the next two downs, they would have been snapping the ball on fourth down to punt with :36 remaining, and with the average punt taking 10 to 13 seconds, the Lions would have received possession of the ball with less than 25 seconds remaining. However, on second down, the Falcons attempted to run the ball again and were flagged for an offensive holding penalty. This stopped the clock following the play, and after an incomplete pass on third down, the Lions ending up receiving possession with 1:38 remaining. Think about that; instead of having less than 25 seconds remaining with no time-outs, the Lions had 1:38 to drive down for a game-winning field goal, which they did shortly thereafter. This demonstrates just how crucial it is for an offense to avoid penalties, or any other clock stoppages, while operating in Pace One.

Another example of improper clock management occurred on November 19, 1978, when Bob Gibson, the offensive coordinator for the New York Giants, decided to run the ball instead of taking a knee during kneel-down time. The unnecessary risk backfired when the running back fumbled the ball and Herm Edwards of the New York Jets returned the fumble for a touchdown to eventually win the game. The lesson to be taken from this game is to not ever stray from the principles of kneel-down time. If a team gets to this point, they should take a knee and avoid any unnecessary risks that may cost them the game. Do not try to prove a point, just take the victory and get to the locker room to avoid an unnecessary potential turnover or injury.

If a defensive team is winning a game in what would be kneel-down time if they had possession of the football, and they get possession via a turnover, it is imperative the ball carrier takes a knee or runs out of bounds immediately. If a defensive team is winning in what would be just outside of kneel-down time, and they obtain possession through a turnover, the ball carrier can run sideways or forward as long as he takes a knee or runs out of bounds before incurring any contact with an opponent that could result in another turnover. He must keep his head on a swivel to ensure he avoids any and all contact.

Often times, teams will take a knee when the game is tied if they are deep in their own end of the football field in order to get to overtime. The question then becomes, when is this a smart decision as opposed to attempting to gain enough yardage to attempt a field goal? The advantage of taking a knee is that it prevents the opponent from forcing a turnover and having an opportunity to score the game-winning points. This is the correct statistical decision when the defense is more likely than the offense to score and the offense has enough downs remaining to run out the rest of the time on the game clock. That is, if the offense has a negative expected value, it would be best for them to take a knee and let the clock expire and resume the game in overtime.

Now, the expected value will vary based on location on the field, down, distance, and time remaining, so it is impossible to create a table to cover each of these scenarios. As a result, it is important to have the strategic assistant calculating the expected values after each play late in the game. However, as a general rule, in order to have a positive expected value, an offense must have a first down with 10 yards to go on at least their opponent's 14 yard line with a minimum of 44 seconds remaining. If these criteria are not met, the offense likely has a negative expected value, and therefore, it would be a better option to take a knee and wait for overtime. However, if the offense does have a positive expected value, they should attempt to gain enough yardage to attempt a field goal because they are more likely to score than their opponents. Taking a knee in that situation would actual benefit the opponent.

SPIKING THE BALL

There has been some debate lately about which option is better for an offense to stop the game clock in the waning moments of a game: spiking the ball or calling a time-out. Generally, an offense will want to avoid spiking the ball whenever they can for two reasons. First, it obviously costs a team a down, which they may need later in the game. This may not be an issue if the offense is already in short field goal range where the teams are tied or the offense is trailing by less than 3 points. However, if the offense is trailing by 3 points or more, they should avoid spiking the ball and wasting a down if possible because their ultimate goal is to score a touchdown to tie or win the game. Wasting a down is also not a consideration if there is not enough time remaining in the half or game to utilize the remaining downs in the series. For example, if it is first down and the game clock is running with 13 seconds remaining in the game, an offense can spike the ball if they do not have a time-out remaining because there is no purpose in saving a down as it will be very unlikely that team will have enough time to run four more plays anyway.

The second reason it is typically more beneficial for an offense to avoid spiking the ball is because from the conclusion of the previous play, it can take anywhere from 11 to 14 seconds for the officials to reset the ball, and the quarterback to hike it and spike it. The inherent problem with spiking the ball is not necessarily the actual play, but rather having the offense properly set in order to snap the ball. Because the offense is generally in a hurry, there is always a risk that the receivers are not in the proper position or the entire offense is not set for the full one second required before the ball is snapped. In these situations, a penalty will be called, which can be devastating to an offense operating in Pace Five. Most of the time, these plays take place in the last minute of the half or game when the offense has no time-outs remaining, and therefore, if a penalty is called as cautioned above, the offense will not only lose 5 yards, but there will also be 10 second run-off of the game clock. This run-off will be incredibly counterproductive for the offense, who could have easily run at least one more play during those 10 seconds. Additionally, many games or halves have ended as a result of the run-off without the offense having an opportunity to snap the ball again.

As a result, in most circumstances, it is more beneficial for a team to use an extra second or two to ensure the entire offense is set in the right positions, instead of risking an offensive penalty. However, an offense should be adequately organized to call a play while the officials are resetting the ball, and for another 2 to 4 seconds, they should be able to snap the ball to execute that called play, instead of just spiking the ball and wasting a down. As discussed earlier, when operating in Pace Five, an offense should try to always have a pre-called play prepared in case they need it in situations like this, and the quarterback should be reminding the offense of that play when the game clock is stopped so it is fresh in everyone's mind when it is needed.

Despite many other experts' opinions, it is no more statistically beneficial to spike the ball on first down, as opposed to second or third down. If an offense is operating in Pace Five, it is ideal that they never face a third down, by achieving a first down prior to doing so; however, if an offense needs to stop the game clock, the quarterback should be able and willing to spike the ball regardless of down, assuming it is not fourth down. If the offense has the option, they should almost always use a time-out instead of spiking the ball. This alternative will save an additional 10 to 13 seconds versus spiking the ball, and there is no chance of a fumble or penalty. As mentioned earlier, do not save a time-out if it is an appropriate time to call one, because you may not need it in the future.

In high school or college, a quarterback should not spike the ball after achieving a first down unless he has no time-outs remaining and there is less than 20 seconds left in the half or game where the offense would not likely have time to run four additional plays anyway. This is because at those two levels, the clock stops after the offense earns a first down while the officials reset the ball, and therefore, the offense can call a play and snap the ball after it is spotted while only using 1 to 2 seconds of the game clock. Finally, if an offense is setting up for a last second field goal to tie or win the game and they have no time-outs remaining, the ball should be spiked with 3 or 4 seconds remaining for the reasons previously stated in Chapter 3.

END OF HALF DECISION

Unfortunately, a lot of head coaches become too conservative near the end of the first half, and decide to take a knee or run the clock out when they potentially could have a chance at scoring some points. Obviously, there will be instances where an offense obtains possession of the football with so little time remaining, that they have no option but to end the half. However, that is not always the case.

Each level has different rules that apply to this situation due to skill level, quarterback arm strength, and a variety of other factors, but as a general rule, if an offense needs to gain less than two yards per second to reach their target, the offense should definitely be running the appropriate plays to achieve that goal. Bear in mind the target can be the end zone, or a spot on the field where an offense believes they have a reasonable opportunity to kick a field goal. Now understand, it is not recommend that an offense be reckless in an effort to reach their target, which is more likely to result in a turnover. But the offense should be operating in Pace 5, and understand the risks and rewards of such a decision.

We previously discussed the importance of each effective possession a team has during a game. With that concept in mind, why would a team want to forego an effective possession just to run out the clock? Coaches and announcers often describe a team running out the remaining time in the first half by stating that the offense is satisfied about their current position in the game. However, that does not justify a team wasting a potential effective possession. Again, the goal of an offense is to score as many points as possible by making the best decisions as measured by each decision's expected value. In these situations, an offense is willingly foregoing potential points because they are worried about the downside. If that was proper logic, a coach would never decide to pass the ball at any time during a game because there is a greater likelihood of a turnover than simply running the ball. A coach is supposed to make the appropriate decision based on the expected value of each decision, and passes are constantly called despite that failed logic because coaches understand that the potential upside of a pass play outweighs the increased risk. That same concept should apply to the end of the first half, and coaches should be more aggressive and understand the benefits of having an extra effective possession.

Another way to look at this situation is to question whether at any other time of a game, would a coach willingly give up an effective possession. Obviously, the answer to that is in the negative. So why has it become acceptable to waste a possession just because the half is concluding? Again, there will be instances where an offense simply does not have enough time to realistically create a scoring opportunity, however, coaches need to understand and implement the analysis behind the proper decision. Additionally, a turnover near the end of the first half could even be less detrimental than one at another point in the game. This is because a defense that creates a turnover near the end of the first half may have less time to take advantage of that turnover with the clock winding down. This is simply another reason why an offense should attempt to score points even if the game clock is winding down in the half if the above requirements are met

QUARTERBACK SNEAKS

Quarterback sneaks have long been a part of football in short yardage situations. Some teams and quarterbacks are much more likely to run such a play, while others seem to shy away from it for fear of injury, turnover, or ineffectiveness. Since 2008, there have been 909 designed quarterback sneaks in the NFL on both third and fourth down. This means that the average team runs a quarterback sneak just over 5 times per year. In college, the numbers are even higher with each team attempting almost six quarterback sneaks per season. The question then becomes, how effective is this play versus calling a traditional running play, or even a pass.

Over the past seven seasons, quarterback sneaks on plays needing less than two yards to gain to achieve a first down have succeeded exactly two-thirds of the time (66.67%). However, when less than one yard is needed to gain the first down, the effective rate of the quarterback sneak balloons to over 83%! Some quarterbacks and offense achieve even more success with this play. For example, Tom Brady and the New England Patriots have attempted the quarterback sneak 119 times on third or fourth down with less than two yards to gain during his tenure with the team, and he has scored a touchdown or gained a first down on 108 of those plays. That is a success rate of almost 91%.

So how does the success of the average quarterback sneak compare with traditional run and pass plays? Over the past same seven seasons, teams not running a quarterback sneak on third or fourth down and less than two yards have succeeded 74.9% of the time, whether they passed or ran the ball. However, when there is less than one yard to gain, the success rate only increases to 81.6%.

As a result of these figures, it appears that when a team has more than one yard to gain for a first down or touchdown, running a traditional play would have a significantly higher success rate, and therefore, a greater expected value than calling a quarterback sneak. Alternatively though, when an offense needs one yard or less to gain, the probability of success is greater when running a quarterback sneak.

Finally, a runner has a slightly higher chance of fumbling on a third or fourth down play when needing two yards or less, whether it be the quarterback or running back carrying the ball. This is likely due to the fact that runners often attempt to leap over the offensive line or expose the ball in an attempt to gain extra yardage, leaving themselves more vulnerable to a fumble. However, I have seen no data that suggests that a quarterback is more likely than a running back to fumble in such a situation, so that was left out of the analysis.

ONSIDE KICKS

In this section, we will take a quick look at the statistical analysis of an onside kick, both when the receiving team is expecting it and when they are not. The reason we split this analysis into two segments is because there is a shocking difference in the probability of success and expected value based on the defense's knowledge that an onside kick is coming. Obviously, when a defense is expecting one, they can prepare accordingly by having receivers, tight ends, and running backs, often referred to as their "hands team," ready to receive such a kick. These are players who have better coordination and typically have better hands to reduce the chance of a fumble. Alternatively, when a receiving team is caught by surprise with an onside kick, some of their front line blockers have already vacated their starting position in order to run back and help block for the returner while anticipating a deep kick. This works to the advantage of the kicking team and increases their chance of recovery. In order to calculate the two segments, we divided onside kicks into two categories, those attempted in the fourth quarter (expected onside kicks), and those attempted in the first three quarters (surprise onside kicks). Even though this is not entirely accurate, as some surprise onside kicks can occur early in the fourth quarter, it will provide the basic statistics for us to analyze.

Now, let's take a look at the expected values to determine if it is proper to attempt a surprise onside kick. In an average NFL season, the kicking team has about a 12.3% chance of recovering an onside kick when the receiving team is expecting it based on NFL data since the 2000 season. On the other hand, if the receiving team is not expecting the onside kick, the success rate balloons to around 47.4% over the same period, and in some statistical windows, can be as high as 59%! Based on the expected value statistics we discuss earlier, if a kicking team in the NFL recovers the onside kick, they will have an expected value of approximately 1.7, assuming they recover the ball immediately after it travels 10 yards. However, if the kick is unsuccessful and the kicking team does not legally recover the ball, the expected value of the kicking team is then -2.1. As we mentioned earlier, a regular kickoff leaves the kicking team with an expected value of -0.7, so that must be factored into the calculation as well, making the true expected value of an unsuccessful onside kick equal to -1.4 by a team foregoing a normal kickoff. We arrive at this calculation by simply subtracting the expected value of a normal kickoff (-0.7) from that of an unsuccessful onside kick (-2.1).

Now, in order to calculate the expected value of the decision to attempt both a surprise and expected onside kick, we must develop a formula like we previously did for fourth down decisions in Chapter 4. The formula we will use is detailed below:

$$(SR \times EVR) + [(1 - SR) \times EVN]$$

SR is equal to the success rate of the onside kick, or the percentage chance the kicking team will recover the onside kick; EVR is the expected value if the kicking team legally recovers the onside kick; and EVN is the expected value of the kicking team if they do not recover the kick. Using the figures for an expected inside kick first, we get the following:

$$(0.123 \times 1.7) + [(1 - 0.123) \times -1.4] = -1.02$$

This result means that every time a kicking team attempts an onside kick that the defense is expecting, they can expect a net scoring result of -1.02 points. This calculation can be somewhat irrelevant though, because when a team is forced to attempt an onside kick because of the lack of time remaining, it is their only option, and expected value is not considered. However, we provide the formula and result here for comparison purposes. Let's now take a look at the statistical figures of a surprise onside kick using the same formula:

$$(0.474 \times 1.7) + [(1 - 0.474) \times -1.4] = 0.07$$

The result of this formula demonstrates that when a kicking team can attempt an onside kick without the receiving team expecting it, they can expect a net scoring difference of 0.07 points. This means that, at least mathematically, a kicking team should attempt an onside kick every time the receiving team is not expecting it, and that will result in a positive expected value. In fact, based on the expected value of a normal kickoff (-0.7), calling a surprise onside kick will have a net benefit of 1.4 points each time it is attempted. Nowadays, most coaches will only attempt an onside kick if they feel they need to "steal" a possession, meaning they are not confident their defense can stop the opposition and they believe their only option to make up points is by their team creating an additional possession through the recovery of an onside kick. However, this analysis proves the opposite is true, and coaches should attempt an onside kick whenever the defense is not prepared for it.

Obviously, a coach cannot attempt this play too often, otherwise the defense will always expect it, and that will change the expected value to a negative number. But, I advise coaches to watch the receiving team throughout the early portion of the game and when reviewing game film of previous games, and by doing so, a coach can usually determine whether or not they are expecting an onside kick on most kickoffs. Finally, it will not be in a team's best interest to attempt an onside kick when they are leading later in the game, as the importance of scoring may decrease as compared to the importance of stopping the opposition from scoring.

When a team is trailing late in a game, experts and media personnel often debate whether a team should try an onside kick or a kickoff and attempt to stop the opposition, thereby forcing a punt. As we previously discussed, a team has a 12.3% chance of recovery of an onside kick when the receiving team is expecting it. In the NFL, each team has a first down probability of 66%, meaning that on average, a team has a 66% chance of earning a first down in a series when they start first and 10. However, late in the game when protecting a lead, the offense has a lesser chance of achieving a first down because they have a somewhat limited playbook due to their desire to have the game clock continue to run after each play. As a result, they often call more running plays and short passes to increase their odds of a completion. In these situations, teams have a first down probability of 59%.

If a kicking team does recover an onside kick though, they will generally have better field position than if they forced the opposition to punt following a normal kickoff. So let's analyze which option would give the kicking team a better chance of obtaining possession and scoring, assuming that if the kicking team allows the receiving team to earn one first down, the receiving team will be in kneel-down time to win the game. As you may recall, an onside kick has an expected value of -1.02. In order to determine the expected value of a deep kickoff, we will use the formula below:

$$(SS \times EVS) + [(1 - SS) \times EVN]$$

SS is the percentage chance of stopping the opposition on their first series of downs; EVS equals the expected value of stopping the opposition and forcing them to punt; and EVN represents the expected value if the kicking allows the receiving team to achieve a first down. Accordingly, we calculate this option as follows:

$$(0.41 \times 0.9) + [(1 - 0.41) \times -1] = -0.22$$

As you can see from these calculations, it is more beneficial to kick off and attempt to stop the opposition than call an onside kick in these situations. However, there are two concepts a coach must consider as well. First, expected value is a little deceiving in this formula because a team in this situation does not care if the opponent scores. Allowing the opponents to gain a first down will guarantee a loss, so this is just as bad as allowing them to score. Second, in some situations, a deep kickoff may not be an option for the kicking team due to the amount of time left. Therefore, the strategic assistant must be sure to analyze each situation so the coach can understand all of the options.

TAKING AN INTENTIONAL SAFETY

Based on the information and games I have seen, many teams do not utilize this weapon as much as they should. As a general rule, teams should only take an intentional safety if they have the lead and giving the opposing team the resulting 2 points from the safety will not change the lead, number of possessions, or type of score it will take the opposition to tie the game or take the lead. Therefore a team should never take a safety if they are leading by more than 8 points, or if they are leading by 1, 2, 4, 5, 7, or 8 points. In all of these situations, a safety will violate the rules against it as stated above. If a team is leading by 3 or 6 points, a safety could be appropriate, but it depends on other circumstances.

For example, if a team is leading by 6 points and they choose to take a safety, they will still be leading by 4 points, in which case a field goal will not be enough to tie the game and a touchdown with the extra point will give the opponent the lead just like if they were still leading by 6 points. Additionally, a team should almost exclusively only take a safety in the fourth quarter, as doing so in any other quarter would be more of a detriment than a potential benefit to a team. The major exception to the rules above would be if the safety would either be the final play of the game, or the second-to-last play where the clock would expire on the subsequent free kick. Whether such a play would be the final play of the game must be calculated based on the distance to the end zone and time remaining on the game clock. This calculation must be evaluated by each coach based on the circumstances.

Both a team's punter and quarterback should be familiar with the process for taking a safety. This should involve turning and sprinting directly into the end zone and stepping out-of-bounds when the opposition gets within a few feet of the ball carrier. It may also be beneficial to have another player familiar with the process, specifically one with good speed in case the line of scrimmage is a farther distance from the team's own end zone, which requires a longer run that must be completed before the defense catches the ball carrier. It is usually also beneficial to run the intentional safety play out of the shotgun formation so the ball carrier will start a couple yards deeper and can have additional time to accomplish what is necessary.

If an offense is facing a fourth down late in the fourth quarter and losing by 4 with possession within their own 20 yard line, it could actually be beneficial to take an intentional safety in this situation. Under these circumstances, a touchdown would still win the game for the defense team, and the offense would get a free kick from the 20 yard line, which would be better field position than a normal punt and without a rush or risk of a blocked punt. Some experts also suggest doing so when a team is trailing by 1 or 5 points because then the team will only need a field goal or touchdown respectively in order to tie the game, although such scores would not win the game as in the previous situations. However, the statistics do not generally support this concept, so I would not recommend doing so. According to such data, the team's win probability would decrease when choosing to take a safety under these circumstances where an offense is trailing by 1 or 5 points.

LETTING THE OPPONENT SCORE

Another situation I would like to cover briefly is when a team should let the opponent score in order to allow themselves enough time for a subsequent drive. I understand that this concept may seem incomprehensible to some coaches. Many argue that you should never let the opponent score because you never know what may happen to prevent them from scoring at all, and a team is essentially giving away points by doing so. However, statistically speaking, there are certain situations when it is in a team's best interest to let their opponents into the end zone. Generally, if a defensive team is winning by 1 or 2 points and the opponent is within chip shot field goal range with the opportunity to effectively utilize all of the remaining time on the clock before attempting the field goal, it may be in a team's best interest to allow the opposition to score a touchdown, which would then put the team down 5 or 6 points, with an opportunity to drive down the field and win the game with a touchdown.

Let us explore the statistics behind this decision to illustrate this point more effectively. First of all, let's assume that a college or NFL team has a 15% chance of scoring a touchdown if they began the possession at their own 20 yard line, which is very close to the average. As a result, allowing an opponent to score a touchdown to take a 5 or 6 point lead would be the correct decision if the opposition was in 'chip-shot' field goal range and had better than an 85% chance of making the field goal. This would mean there was a greater chance of the defense winning by scoring a touchdown on the ensuing drive as opposed to the trailing team missing the field goal attempt. So when do kickers have less than an 85% chance of making the field goal? In the NFL, a kicker will successfully convert a field goal at least 85% of the time from inside of 35 yards. This means that if the line of scrimmage is within a team's 18 yard line when they are leading by 1 or 2, it would be statistically more beneficial to let the opponent score a touchdown and attempt to win the game on their subsequent drive.

Again, this is only done when the offense has the opportunity to effectively utilize the remaining game clock prior to attempting the field goal. Otherwise, a defense leading the game can still try to stop the offense, and if they are unsuccessful, they can utilize the remaining time to attempt to drive the field for a game-winning touchdown. When the difference in the game is exactly 3 points, there is no reason to allow the opponent to score a touchdown because if the defensive team is able to hold the offense to a field goal, the worst they can do is end regulation in a tie.

This strategy can also be used when a team is trailing by 1 point. Let's assume Team A is losing 21–20 with no time-outs remaining and Team B has possession of the ball on Team A's 5 yard line with 2:30 left and are facing a first down and goal. Under these circumstances, although Team B is not yet in kneel-down time, they should be running plays in order to use up the game clock without actually scoring. If Team B can run three plays that allow the clock to continue to run, which should be QB sweeps as discussed earlier in this chapter, Team B could kick a field goal on fourth down and leave Team A between 2 and 25 seconds left depending on the length of the plays and whether there is a 2-minute warning. In this situation, if Team B runs a play, it would be in Team A's best interest to allow Team B to score and try to tie the game on the ensuing drive with a touchdown and 2-point conversion.

As mentioned earlier, an offense has about a 15% chance of scoring a touchdown on the following possession. On average, a team has about a 50% probability of successfully converting a 2-point conversion, and if that is accomplished, the game will likely be determined in overtime, where each team would have approximately a 50% chance of winning.

Therefore, in the situation above where Team A allows Team B to score, Team A would then have approximately a 3.75% chance of scoring a touchdown on their next drive, converting the 2-point conversion, and winning the game in overtime. Although this is not a great probability, if Team B does not score and utilizes the game clock as they should, Team A's winning percentage will be at or near 0%, meaning allowing Team B to score could be the only chance Team A has of winning.

The closest example of this play that most people remember is Super Bowl XXXII between the Packers and the Broncos. In that game, the Packers were leading 24–23 with 1:48 remaining, and the Broncos had possession of the ball, facing a second and goal from the Packers 1 yard line. The Packers decided to let them score but failed to score a touchdown on their ensuing drive, thereby losing the game. But was this the right decision? In this situation, the Packers had two time-outs remaining, so assuming they could have kept the Broncos out of the end zone on the next two plays, they could have called their final two time-outs after each of those plays, and even if the Broncos made the field goal attempt, the Packers would have had approximately 1:30 remaining, only needing a field goal to win the game. Therefore, in this situation, the call to let them score was incorrect. However, if the Packers would have had zero or possibly one time-out remaining, it would have been the correct call. While I doubt the Packers coach, Mike Holmgren, had the appropriate data to understand the correct call, I did like that a coach was able to make the courageous call to let the opponent score, even if it wasn't the correct decision in this case. More coaches should consider this option when the circumstances present themselves as discussed above.

TWO-POINT CONVERSIONS

There has been a lot of discussion surrounding the 2-point conversion since its inception in the NFL in 1994, and even before that with its existence in college football since 1958. Some experts believe a team should always attempt a 2-point conversion after a touchdown because it has a higher expected value than simply kicking an extra point. In this section, we are going to evaluate the expected value of a 2-point conversion versus an extra point to determine which is the best option for an offense following a touchdown; we will also discuss when a 2-point conversion should be attempted.

After the initial edition of this book was published, the NFL modified the rules governing an extra point. Prior to 2015, an extra point amounted to essentially a 20-yard field goal. The kickers in the NFL were successful on extra point attempts over 98% of the time under the old NFL rules. As a result of the new rules, an extra point being kicked is snapped from the 15-yard line, resulting in what equates to a 33-yard field goal attempt.

Based on data from the last 10 seasons prior to the 2015 rule change, the success rate of a 2-point conversion in the NFL was approximately 47.7%. Meanwhile, the success rate of a kicked extra point was about 98.4%. Now, let's calculate the expected value of each option like we did with the fourth down options in the last chapter. In order to do so, we will use the following formula:

$$(SR \times EVS) + [(1 - SR) \times EVN]$$

SR equals the success rate of the attempt; EVS represents the expected value of a successful 2-point conversion attempt; and EVN equals the expected value of an unsuccessful attempt. Using the data discussed above, we get the following result for the expected value of a 2-point conversion attempt in the NFL:

$$(0.477 \times 2) + [(1 - 0.477) \times 0] = 0.954$$

These results demonstrate that when an NFL team attempts a 2-point conversion, they have an expected value of 0.954 points. Obviously, a team cannot score 0.954 points, so another way to view it is for every 1,000 2-point conversion attempts, a team will be successful an average of 477 times, which equals 954 points. Now let's examine the expected value of a traditional kicked extra point under the old NFL rules. Using the same formula, we get the following result:

$$(0.984 \times 1) + [(1 - 0.984) \times 0] = 0.984$$

This calculation shows that a team attempting a traditional extra point has an expected value of 0.984 points per try, or for every 1,000 tries, they will be successful 984 times, which would earn them 984 points. Based on this analysis, after a touchdown was scored in the NFL, the average team should have attempted a traditional kicked extra point prior to 2015, except in special situations that we will discuss shortly.

But, does this calculation change with the increased distance of the extra point. Since the new rule has been implemented, the success rate of an extra point in the NFL has decreased to 94.2% in the limited sample size we have thus far. Using the same formula detailed above, we can calculate the new expected value of kicking an extra point in the NFL as follows:

$$(0.942 \times 1) + [(1 - 0.942) \times 0] = 0.942$$

Based on the expected value of kicking the extra point (.942), the alternative with the higher expected value under the new NFL rule is attempting the two-point conversion. Again, the expected value of the two point conversion was .954. This means that if the average NFL team went for a two point conversation instead of kicking an extra point after every touchdown, they would score slightly more points over the course of the season (approximately 1.2 points), thus making it the correct option according to the expected value calculation. Obviously, there are situations where it still would not be the best choice. For example, if a team just scored a touchdown to tie the game with under a minute remaining, it would be more beneficial to attempt a kicked extra point since the second point would not increase a team's win probability at all. However, according to the statistics, after the average touchdown, an NFL team should be attempting a two point conversation every time, and it appears many teams are beginning to understand this concept. The amount of two point conversions has almost doubled in 2015 as compared to the 2014 season.

Now we are going to use the same formula to determine the results for a college football team. On average, a college team is successful approximately 42.3% of the time when attempting a 2-point conversion, and about 96.9% of the extra point attempts. Using the formula outlines previously, we get the following results:

$$\text{2-Point Conversion: } (0.423 \times 2) + [(1 - 0.423) \times 0] = 0.846$$
$$\text{Extra Point: } (0.969 \times 1) + [(1 - 0.969) \times 0] = 0.969$$

As you can see, it would generally be more beneficial for a college team to attempt an extra point given the lower success rate on 2-point conversion attempts. Finally, we will evaluate the data at the high school level as well. As a disclaimer, the skill level of kickers at the high school level varies so greatly that this calculation may not apply to all teams. Again, we will use what we believe to be the data of an average high school, and in doing so, we get the following results:

$$\text{2-Point Conversion: } (0.416 \times 2) + [(1 - 0.401) \times 0] = 0.832$$
$$\text{Extra Point: } (0.828 \times 1) + [(1 - 0.828) \times 0] = 0.828$$

Based on this calculation, the data demonstrates that for an average high school football team, it would be more beneficial to attempt a 2-point conversion after every touchdown, although there is not a huge difference. As stated before, this result will differ significantly based on the skill level of a high school team's kicker, so it is important for a coaching staff to calculate the options covered above for their respective teams.

I also wanted to quickly touch on the situation where there is a defensive penalty on the extra point try, resulting in the ball being spotted half the distance to the goal. In these situations, the success rate of a 2-point conversion will increase significantly, roughly 16 to 18% for each level. Based on this information, we get the following result when utilizing the expected value formula containing the NFL information:

$$\text{2-Point Conversion: } (0.645 \times 2) + [(1 - 0.645) \times 0] = 1.29$$
$$\text{Extra Point: } (0.942 \times 1) + [(1 - 0.942) \times 0] = 0.942$$

As you can see from these calculations, a defensive penalty resulting in the ball being placed half the distance to the goal will have a large impact on the expected value of the 2-point conversion, making it always beneficial to attempt such a conversion unless it is late in the game as discussed below and there would be no additional benefit obtaining that second point awarded for the 2-point conversion. The same is true at the lower levels as the increased success rate will control the results, recommending that a team always attempt the 2-point conversion at the college and high school levels. Assessing the same defensive penalty on the ensuing kickoff would have a much smaller effect on the kicking team's expected value, decreasing the number from -.7 to -6.89. Therefore, it would be more beneficial to accept the penalty on the PAT attempt and try a 2-point conversion.

Another unique situation deals with when a team is driving for a touchdown late in the game while leading by one point. Assuming they score a touchdown, the decision becomes should the offense kick the extra point to lead by eight forcing the opposition to score a touchdown and 2-point conversion to tie the game, or should the offense attempt a 2-point conversion to lead by nine points and essentially end the game. But if they are unsuccessful, the opposition will only need a touchdown and kicked an extra point to tie the game. In order to calculate and compare these alternatives, we will use the following formula for when an NFL offense chooses to attempt a kicked extra point:

$$[XPS \times (1 - PT8)] + [XPU \times (1 - PT7)]$$

XPS equals the percentage chance the extra point is successful; PT8 represents the likelihood of the opposition tying the game when trailing by eight points; XPU equals the percentage chance the extra point attempt is unsuccessful; and PT7 represents the likelihood that a defense will tie the game when trailing by seven points. Using the data from applicable situations in NFL games over the past 15 season, we get the following results:

$$[.942 \times (1 - .1018)] + [.058 \times (1 - .2011)] = .8923 \text{ or } 89.23\%$$

Therefore, if an NFL team scores a touchdown after already leading by one point with the opposition having no more than one possession remaining, and they attempt to kick the extra point, the scoring team has 89.23% chance the defense will not tie or take the lead on the ensuing possession. Now we will utilize the same formula to see what the results are if the offense chose to attempt a 2-point conversion:

$$[.477 \times (1-0)] + [.523 \times (1 - .2011)] = .8948 \text{ or } 89.48\%$$

As a result of this calculation, if the scoring team chose to attempt a 2-point conversion following the touchdown in the same scenario, that team would have a 89.48% chance of winning without the opposition tying or taking the lead on the ensuing possession, which is just slightly higher than kicking the extra point.

With the 2-point conversion being around for a significant period of time, most coaches, if not all, have memorized the chart below, which listed the appropriate situations in which to attempt a 2-point conversion prior to the NFL rule change.

TWO POINT CONVERSION TABLE

Attempt a 2-point conversion when trailing by:	2, 5, 10
Attempt a 2-point conversion when leading by:	1, 4, 5

The figures contained in the table above apply after a team has been awarded the 6 points for the touchdown. However, as discussed earlier, this chart no longer applies to NFL teams as the statistics show that a team should almost always be attempting a two-point conversion, and the same applies to high school teams. Therefore, the following information only applies to collegiate teams and high schools with above-average kickers.

It is appropriate to attempt a 2-point conversion when the resulting extra point will allow a team to tie the game or reduce or increase the number of possessions the trailing team will need to tie the game. We have all heard commentators and coaches state that it was too early to try for the 2-point conversion, and most of the time, they are correct. In most situations in the first three quarters, it is not worth the risk to attempt a 2-point conversion because the expected value is less than kicking the extra point as analyzed above. So, the real question becomes how late in a game a team should implement the table above. As discussed before, the average possession in the fourth quarter is just under 2:30. Based on this fact, a team should be implementing the 2-point conversion chart when there is less than 7:25 remaining in the fourth quarter. The reason for this is because based on the average length of a possession, the offensive team attempting the PAT may only have one more possession in the game, assuming the teams alternate possessions. The table above is most applicable when each team has one possession remaining and points become increasingly important.

MISCELLANEOUS LATE GAME PLAYS

In college and the NFL, the defense can also score two points by return-ing an extra point or two-point conversion to the opponent's end zone. Therefore, in the last minute of the game, a coach must weigh the risk and reward of attempting an extra point or 2-point conversion. For example, if a team scores a touchdown to take a 1 point lead before attempting the extra point, and there is less than a minute left, the chart says the offense should "go for two" in order to make it a 3 point lead, where a field goal would only tie the game instead of taking the lead. However, if the offense is intercepted or fumbles on the conversion attempt, they could end up losing the game if the defense returns the turnover for two points. As a result, coaches must be aware of this situation and make the appropriate play call to limit the chance of this happening. Quarterbacks must also be cognizant of this, as it may be better to take a sack versus throwing a dangerous pass that can be intercepted.

As discussed previously, it generally takes the officials 11 to 13 seconds to reset the ball after a play. Accordingly, if the offensive team is tied or trailing late in the game, does not have any time-outs remaining, and the ball carrier cannot get out-of-bounds to set up for a last-second field goal or Hail Mary, he should gain as much yardage as possible and take a knee with 15 to 17 seconds left to allow enough time for the refs to reset the ball and the offense to have one last play. It is also important for the ball car-rier to hand or toss the ball to the official to reduce the amount of time it takes to reset for the following play. Placing the ball on the ground could result in it being kicked or moved by the defense, which would waste valu-able time. The average time of a pass play is 5 to 7 seconds, so if the ball is snapped with more than 20 to 23 seconds remaining, do not be afraid to pass the ball over the middle as long as the receiver is aware he must take a knee as described above. The offense also must know how much time they would need to get their field goal unit on the field or set up their receivers for one final play.

Additionally, in high school and the NFL, there is a little known and rarely used rule allowing a team receiving a punt to opt for a free kick from the spot where it is received. To utilize this rule, the receiver must signal for a fair catch prior to catching the ball. If he does so, the receiving team's kicker can attempt a free kick, where there will be no holder or snapper, and the defense will have to stand at least 10 yards away from the spot, even if there is no time remaining on the clock. This free kick is also beneficial because there is no snap or rush, so the kicker will not have to stand 6 to 7 yards behind the line of scrimmage like a typical field goal, making it a shorter kick. Again, this is rarely used because the situation doesn't often present itself; however, if a team is tied or trailing by 3 points or less and the opposition is punting from deep within their own territory, it may be something to keep in mind. A receiving team will need to remind its receiver to fair catch the kick. For the punting team, the way to prevent this play is to kick the ball out-of-bounds. As a result, the receiver could not fair catch the ball and there would be no opportunity for a free kick.

CHAPTER 5 SUMMARY

- Coaches should be familiar with their kicker's skills and preferences in order to prepare accordingly for a late field goal.
- Time-outs and spike plays to set up for a last-second field goal should be done with 3 or 4 seconds remaining in order to ensure the clock expires during the field goal, and an additional time-out can be called in case of a bad snap or fumble in order to attempt another kick.
- If a team gains enough yardage to be within field goal range, a coach should continue to operate his offense to gain yardage and increase the probability of a successful field goal attempt, or even score a touchdown.
- A team's chances of a successful Hail Mary play increase as the offense nears the end zone.
- A team will have a better chance of a successful Hail Mary or lateral play if it is not the last play of the game. If a team is in Hail Mary range, it will be more beneficial in some situations to attempt two Hail Mary passes as opposed to try to gain yardage prior to a final Hail Mary play.
- In order to defend a Hail Mary, a defense should attempt to knock the ball out-of-bounds where it cannot be legally caught.
- A team should always have a lateral play in their playbook that involves a long lateral across the field. When defending a lateral play, a defense should be sure to stay in their lanes to defend against such a lateral.
- When a team is in kneel-down time, they should avoid running any other plays. If a team is just outside of kneel-down time, the offense should execute quarterback sweep plays to use additional time.
- Spiking the ball to stop the clock should be a last resort because it wastes a down and a pre-called play could be run using just a few more seconds.

- Offensive coaches need to be more aggressive with the final possession of the first half if the offense needs to gain less than two yards per second to reach their target.
- Quarterback sneaks are generally more successful than traditional plays when an offense needs to gain one yard or less.
- Onside kicks should be utilized more by coaches when not expected by the defense because of their increased success rate and higher expected value than a traditional kickoff.
- If a team is trailing late in the game with the appropriate amount of time remaining, that team generally has a higher expected value kicking off and trying to force a punt rather than attempting an onside kick, for which the receiving team is prepared.
- In general, teams should only consider taking an intentional safety if they have the lead and giving the opposing team the 2 points from the safety will not change the lead, number of possessions, or type of score it will take the opposition to tie the game or take the lead.
- A coach should allow the opposition to score if they are leading by 1 point late in the game and the opponent's field goal probability is greater than the chances of scoring a touchdown on their next possession.
- In the NCAA, the expected value of an extra point is greater than the expected value of a 2-point conversion. However, due to recent rule changes, in the NFL, along with most high schools, teams have a higher expected value attempting a 2-point conversion.
- The 2-point conversion table should be implemented with less than 7:25 remaining in a college game based on the average length of possession in the fourth quarter.

Chapter 6

SPECIAL TEAMS

IN GENERAL, SPECIAL teams have a correlation factor of about 18%, which means that, on average, special teams contribute about 18% to whether a team wins or loses a given game. As a result, I wanted to dedicate a chapter to special teams and delve into a little more detail on the different decisions that commonly arise in this aspect of the game. In Chapter 4, we covered several expected value formulas that help determine when it is appropriate for an offense to punt or kick a field goal. So we are not going to address those options and decisions in much more detail in this chapter; however, we will cover a few more topics and decisions that are made by special team coaches and players. For example, is there any benefit to attempting a fake punt or field goal, and when should such a play be called? We will also discuss if a player should return a kickoff that travels into the end zone, and what type of return should be expected based on the average of similar returns. Finally, we will cover the average returns of kickoffs and punts and how that can impact a team's expected value.

KICKOFF RETURNS

As we addressed previously, the average starting field position in the NFL following a kickoff is the receiving team's own 22 yard line. In college, the average starting field position increases slightly to the 27 yard line, and finally in high school, it improves even further to the 29 yard line. In high school, a lot of states have different rules governing kickoffs, specifically that once a kickoff crosses the plane of the end zone, it is automatically a touchback. Therefore, when we discuss whether a player should return a kickoff out of the end zone, this obviously would not apply to high school teams and games governed by such a rule.

As an introductory note, all of the data used in the following analysis for kickoffs is derived from the 2011 season through the present for NFL kickoffs, and from 2012 to the present for college kickoffs. This is because that is when these levels changed the point of the kickoff from the kicking team's 30 yard line to the 35 yard line in order to decrease the number of returns, and hopefully, potential injuries as well. Obviously, moving the kickoff forward has had a tremendous impact on a lot of the statistics, and therefore, only data since those years will be used in this analysis. Since the 2011 season, approximately 81% of the kickoffs in the NFL have traveled into the end zone, and since 2012, almost 69% of college kickoffs have done so. As you would imagine, this is significantly higher than the percentage prior to moving the kickoff forward 5 yards.

The question then becomes, how deep are these kicks traveling into the end zone on an average basis? We first need to incorporate this data because, presumably, that will affect the starting field position of the return team. Common sense would have you believe that the deeper a returner started in the end zone, the worse the starting field position would be for his team. Before we address this concept, we are going to review some kickoff data. First, we are going to disregard the kickoffs that travel out of the end zone or bounce into the end zone because these kicks are generally unreturnable, and therefore, there is no decision to make for the receiving team. Out of the returnable kicks that traveled into the end zone and were caught by the receiver, the chart below details exactly how deep in the end zone the ball is traveling on NFL kickoffs since 2011:

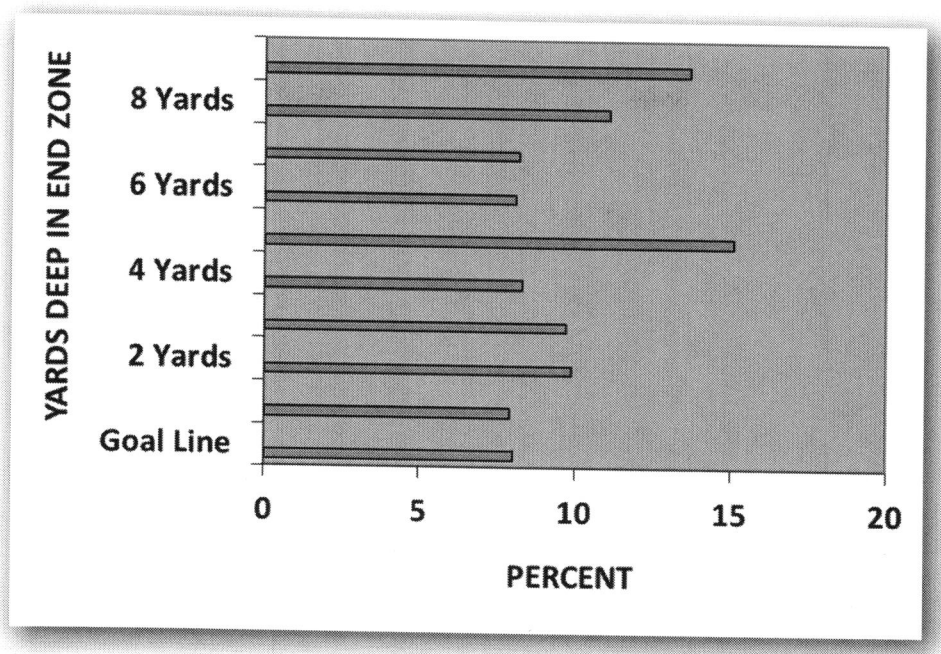

As you can see from the chart above, the distance of the kick varies greatly and is relatively evenly distributed. The only distance at which the ball landed over 15% of the time was 5 yards deep in the end zone, and the difference between the most common and least common distance was just over 7%. Now, let's take a look at the same chart but for collegiate kickoffs since 2012:

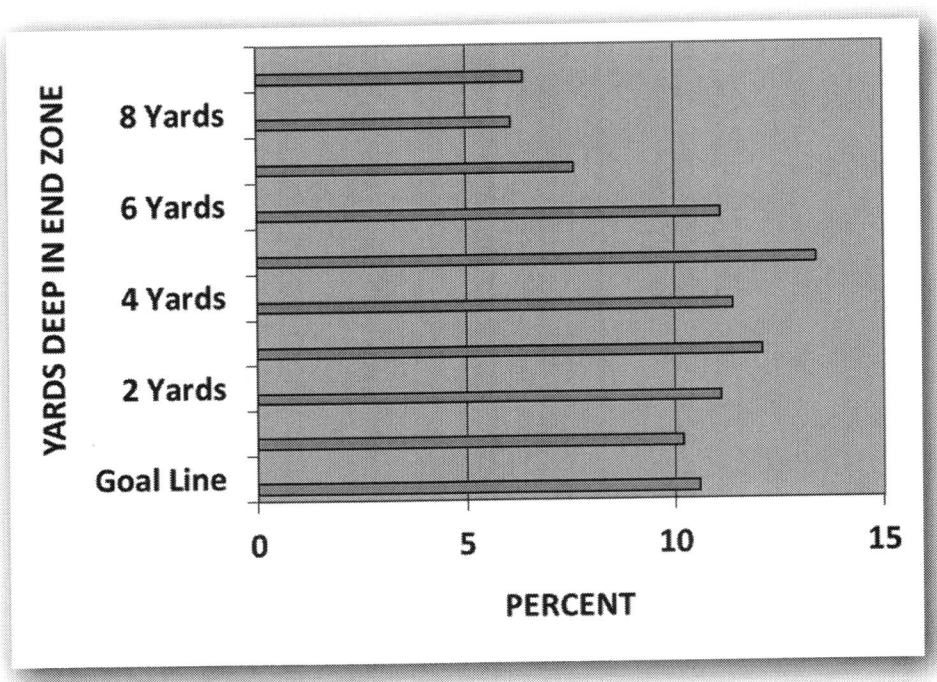

Looking at the same chart for collegiate kickers, we can see there are a couple patterns that did not appear in the NFL chart. First of all, there seems to be a greater variance as the difference between the most common and least common distance is higher than that of the NFL. Additionally, the percentage of kicks that traveled deeper than 6 yards into the end zone is relatively low. In the NFL, about 33% of kicks traveled more than 6 yards into the end zone, while in college, that figure dropped to about 20.1%. This is most likely due to some college kickers not having the kicking strength to consistently kick the ball as far as NFL kickers, who can routinely do so.

Now that we have this information, we are going to take a look at the attempted returns out of the end zone from each distance and the result of those returns. In order to do that, we are first going to take a look at the frequency at which returners take the kick out of the end zone. The following chart breaks down the amount of time a kickoff is returned out of the end zone based on where the ball was caught, as a percentage of total kickoffs caught in the end zone, for both the NFL and NCAA. Once we have this information, we can discuss the average return distance from each starting position, the subsequent initial field position, and whether it is beneficial for receivers to return kicks from the end zone based on their starting point. This information will allow coaches to instruct returners when it is appropriate and advantageous to return kicks versus when accepting a touchback would be more beneficial, and allow the offense better starting field position, and therefore, a higher expected value.

PERCENTAGE OF NFL KICKOFFS RETURNED FROM END ZONE	
GOAL LINE	12.6%
1 YARD DEEP	11.8%
2 YARDS DEEP	12.9%
3 YARDS DEEP	13.5%
4 YARDS DEEP	11.2%
5 YARDS DEEP	16.6%
6 YARDS DEEP	8.1%
7 YARDS DEEP	5.4%
8 YARDS DEEP	5.8%
9 YARDS DEEP	2.1%

As you can see from the table above, in the vast percentage of instances when a kickoff is taken out of the end zone by a returner, it traveled less than 6 yards deep. This represents almost 80% of the kickoffs that were returned, and it is relatively evenly distributed throughout all of those depths.

However, once the ball traveled 6 yards or deeper into the end zone, the chance of it being returned significantly decreased to almost half as often, totaling only about 21.4% of the time. Logically, that would seem to be predictable given that the deeper the receiver starts his return in the end zone, the less likely he should be able to reach at least the 20 yard line, which would make it beneficial to return the kick. Now, we are going to take a look at the same table for NCAA kickoffs since 2012 to see if there is any significant difference from the NFL table, as there was with the kickoff distance.

PERCENTAGE OF NCAA KICKOFFS RETURNED FROM END ZONE	
GOAL LINE	15.6%
1 YARD DEEP	14.9%
2 YARDS DEEP	17.2%
3 YARDS DEEP	13.5%
4 YARDS DEEP	14.4%
5 YARDS DEEP	9.4%
6 YARDS DEEP	6.0%
7 YARDS DEEP	3.5%
8 YARDS DEEP	3.9%
9 YARDS DEEP	1.6%

Looking at the NCAA table, there are similarities to the NFL data. First of all, the returns are consistently related to kickoffs that travel 4 yards or less into the end zone, and those distances account for almost 70% of the returns. However, there are some differences as well, such as a significantly lower percentage of returns from the 6 to 9 yard deep range. This is most likely due to the lesser amount of kicks that are traveling that distance in college, but it also indicates a receiver's unwillingness to take a chance returning the kickoff from that deep into the end zone.

Now that we have that information, we can begin analyzing it to determine if and when it is advantageous for a receiver to return a kick from the end zone. First of all, we must address the possibility of a penalty or turnover. In general, a penalty on the kickoff occurs approximately 17.1% of the time in the NFL and during about 15.6% of the kickoffs in the NCAA. In order to account for this possibility, this data is factored into the calculation on average starting field position that we are about to discuss, so the chance of a penalty being called on a particular return is included. Additionally, a returner fumbles about 2.8% of his returns, with the kicking team recovering the ball about 64% of the time it is fumbled by the returner, or on about 1.8% of total kickoffs. We will incorporate this data into the expected values that we calculate shortly.

To begin analyzing this data, let's now take a look at the average starting field position of the returning team when a kick is brought out of the end zone. Below is a graph providing this information broken down by how deep in the end zone the returner receives the kick in the NFL.

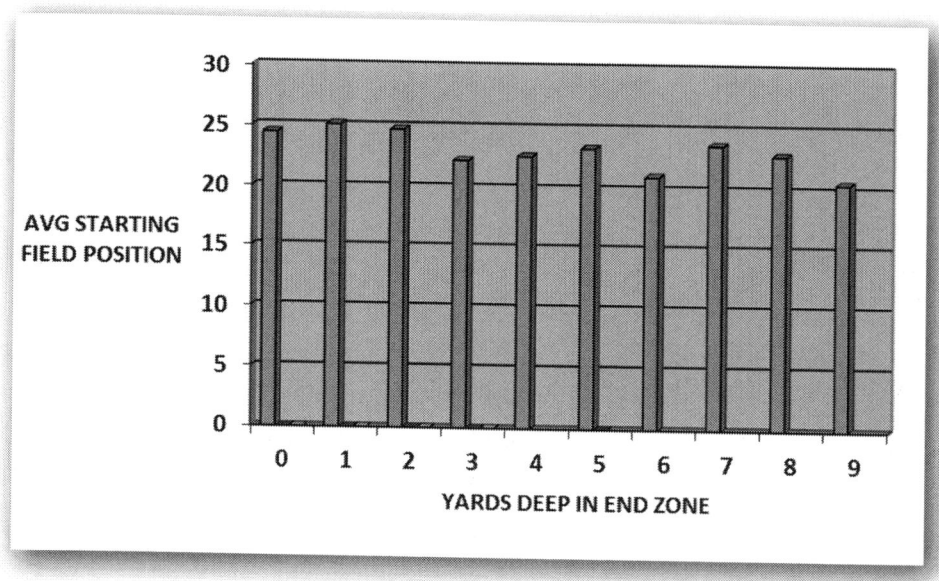

Based on the kickoffs returned from the end zone since the 2011 NFL season, and accounting for the starting field position after all penalties are assessed, it appears as though it does not matter how deep a returner receives the kick; it is always beneficial to bring the kick out of the end zone because the average starting field position will be past the 20 yard line, giving the offense better field position than simply accepting a touchback. The average starting field position is remarkably similar for college football as well, so we will use this same chart for both levels.

The reason many coaches do not want their returners taking the ball out of the end zone is because they are worried about bad field position, such as inside their own 10 yard line. First, that data would be included in the calculation used to produce the graph above, and the results still say that, utilizing the data we have covered so far, it is still beneficial for the returner to bring the ball out of the end zone. Second, we will now take a look at how often a team ends up with a starting field position inside their own 10 yard line after returning a kick from their own end zone. For kickoffs fielded less than 5 yards deep in the end zone, a returner rarely does not make it back to his 10 yard line. On average, less than 1% of the time does the returner get tackled within his own 10 yard line when fielding the ball less than 5 yards deep in the end zone.

Even when a returner fields the ball 5 to 9 yards deep in his end zone, he still only gets tackled inside his own 10 yard line about 4.52% of time. Therefore, it is a rarity that a returning team will have terrible starting field position barring a penalty, which was factored into the calculations above. Now, what does occur more often is a returner not making it back to his 20 yard line, thus giving the offense worse starting field position than if the receiver took a knee for a touchback; however, this does not reduce an offense's expected value much, and that is part of the price that must be paid for the opportunity to have a big return. In order to compare the benefit and detriment of such a decision, we are now going to take a look at the expected value of the decision to return a kickoff out of the end zone, which as we have discussed before, will provide an overall calculation of whether it is advantageous to do so.

In order to calculate the expected value of returning the kickoff from each point in the end zone, we are going to take the expected value of the average return, which already accounts for the possibility of a penalty, and factor in the chance and result of a turnover. Accordingly, the formula we will use to calculate the expected value is:

$$EVA + (PT \times EVT)$$

EVA equals the expected value of the average return; PT represents the chance of a turnover; and EVT equals the expected value of the opponent after recovering the turnover. We will calculate the expected value of a return from each yard deep in the end zone using the formula described above and compare that to the expected value of a touchback to determine what would be the better option for each distance that a kickoff may travel into the end zone. The results of these calculations are depicted in the following graph:

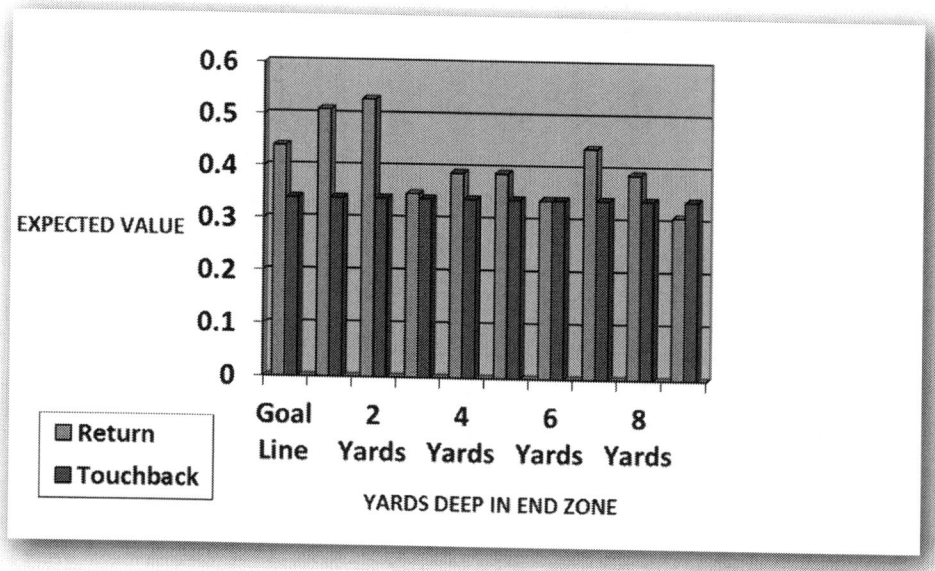

As you can see from the graph above, the expected value of returning the kick in the NFL is equal to or greater than the expected value of a touchback, accounting for the possibility of a penalty or turnover, except when the kick travels 9 yards deep in the end zone. Therefore, it would be beneficial for the receiver to return the ball in every scenario, other than when the kickoff travels 9 yards deep in the end zone, based on the averages and calculation contained herein.

In college, even though the average starting field position based on the distance the kickoff traveled is very similar to the NFL, the results of the expected value analysis is somewhat different because in the NCAA, the field position following a touchback is the 25 yard line, as opposed to the 20 yard line of the NFL. As a result, the expected value of a touchback would be higher in college football, which may make returning the kickoff out of the end zone less beneficial. The chart below displays the corresponding results for college football using the same formula we utilized previously for the NFL analysis:

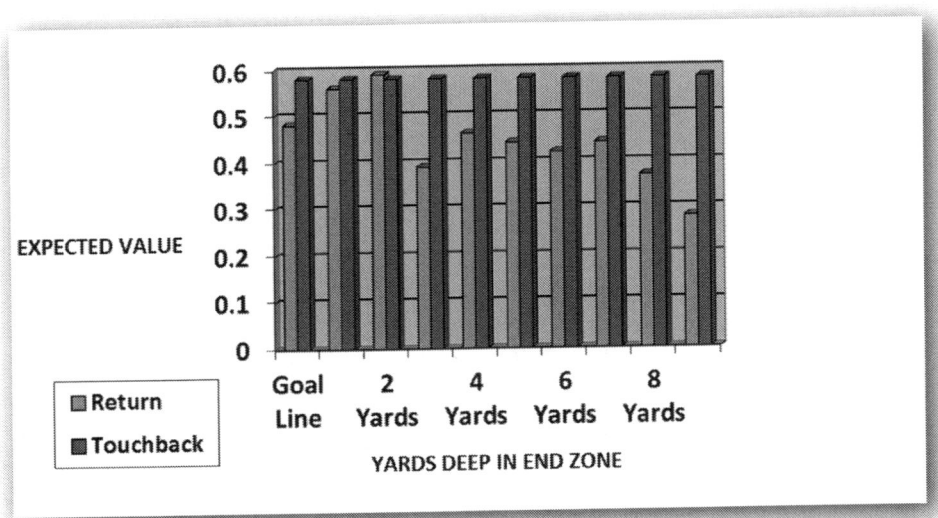

As you can see from this chart, the extra 5 yards given to the receiving team for a touchback makes a significant difference in the expected value calculation. Based on the calculations, in college, it is not nearly as advantageous to return the kick when the kickoff travels less than 4 yards deep into the end zone. Even then, the only actual advantage of returning the kickoff is a slight one when the ball is caught 2 yards deep in the end zone. I would recommend to college coaches to be more willing to accept a touchback unless that team has a significantly above-average returner or the game situation dictates a different decision.

Obviously, these charts only apply to the typical circumstances and do not take into account which team is winning, the amount of time remaining in the game, and the skilled returners whose average kickoff returns are significantly higher than the rest of the league. Late in the game, especially when the receiving team is trailing, it would be beneficial to return a kickoff with the hope and possibility of a long return, or even touchdown, knowing that the receiving team is desperate and a bad return or turnover will not alter the win probability very much. In these situations, the coach and returner must be willing to take additional chances, and both individuals should be aware of the appropriate time to do so. This decision will be dictated by the win probability of the receiving team at the time of the kickoff, and the strategic assistant should be able to communicate this to both individuals when the situation is appropriate

Since the kickoff rules have changed in 2011 for the NFL and 2012 for the NCAA, touchbacks have increased significantly, as was the intent of the rule. Touchbacks in the NFL have increased almost 30%, and the same has occurred in college by about 20%. How has that changed the amount of returns that result in touchdowns? Interestingly, the NFL and NCAA have experienced different results. Prior to the rule changes, both levels saw approximately 1% of returns, not kickoffs, result in touchdowns. However, since the rule change, the NFL touchdown percentage has decreased to about 0.71%, meaning that only about 1 out of every 140 kickoff returns results in a touchdown in the NFL. Conversely, the touchdown percentage in the NCAA has increased to nearly 1.3%, meaning that now roughly 1 out of 77 kickoff returns will result in a touchdown. This is a relatively small sample size given that the rules just changed a couple years ago, but we will continue to monitor these results.

On the other hand, punts are almost twice as likely to result in a touchdown at both levels but also have an increased chance of a penalty called against the returning team. In the NFL, punts are returned for touchdowns approximately 1.47% of the time, more than twice as likely as a kickoff. Similarly, in college, punt returns result in touchdowns about 2.5% of the time. There are a couple of reasons why a greater percentage of punts are returned for touchdowns than kickoffs. First, when punting, a lot depends on whether the kicking coverage team can get a good release from the line of scrimmage. The majority of the team must hold back and block the defenders until the punt is released, thereby preventing them from leaving too quickly. On kickoffs, the kicking team does not have to worry about blocking the receiving team and the coverage team has no opponent directly in their way when they leave the line of scrimmage. Second, on a kickoff, the coverage team can spread the field and stay in their lanes in order to reduce the open space available to the returner, while on a punt, there are more holes that open because of the reasons stated above. Finally, kickoffs must often be returned 90 to 105 yards in order score a touchdown, while some punts can simply be returned 50 to 75 yards in order for the returner to score. As a result, all of these factors work together to lead to an increased amount of punts ending in touchdowns.

As mentioned previously, penalties are also called more frequently on punts as opposed to kickoffs. This is again due to the amount of action that occurs prior to the receiver catching the ball on a punt. For example, blockers often hold the "gunner" on a punt in order to create time for the returner, which often does not happen on kickoffs due to the free release of the coverage players during a kickoff. In the NFL, penalties are called on the receiving team during punts about 21.7% of the time, where penalties are only called about 17.1% of the plays during kickoffs. College football experiences a similar increase, with a punt resulting in a penalty 19.5% of the time, as opposed to 15.6% for kickoffs. The reason I mention this is because penalties can often result in worse field position for the receiving team than if they just simply called a fair catch every punt.

For example, the average punt return in the NFL over the last three seasons was just over 8.5 yards. However, with penalties being called on the return team about 21.7% of the punts, commonly resulting in a loss of 10 yards, the question then becomes what the expected value of a punt return is for the receiving team, factoring in the possibility of a penalty or turnover. In order to do this, we will use the calculation below to determine the increase or decrease in expected value by choosing to return a punt versus simply calling a fair catch. The equation we will use for this calculation is below:

$$(PN \times EVAR) + (PP \times EVP) + (PT \times EVT)$$

PN represents the percentage of time the return stands where no penalty or turnover occurs; EVAR is the increase in expected value of that average return; PP represents the percentage chance there is a penalty called on the receiving team; EVP equals the decrease in expected value when a penalty is called; PT represents the percentage of time there is a turnover by the returner recovered by the punting team; and EVT equals the expected value of the receiving team when a turnover occurs.

When we run this calculation based on the average NFL statistics we have discussed, the result is 0.206, which shows that despite the chances of a penalty or turnover, choosing to return a punt will increase the receiving team's expected value by 0.206 points, meaning that returning the punt is more beneficial than simply signaling for a fair catch every return as some experts have suggested. Also, bear in mind that this calculation was based on the average return, meaning that if a kick travels farther than usual or a returner receives it deeper in his own territory, this number can change, although it will not be significant.

FAKE PLAYS

Next, we will cover fake field goals and fake punts to determine whether they are worth the risk. Some analysts have argued against such plays, suggesting that simply running a play with a team's normal offensive personnel would be more effective. However, running a fake attempt also means the defense does not generally have the correct personnel on the field to stop the play, nor are they likely in the correct formation. In order to address these points, let's take a look at the statistics to determine if there is a benefit to these plays.

There is not too much data on these plays, given that they are somewhat rare. In fact, since 2000, it appears that there has been less than 250 fake field goal and fake punt attempts in the NFL. That is an average of about 16 to 17 per season. As a result, the data may be slightly skewed given the small sample size, but we will take a look at it based on the data we have and evaluate the results of such. Obviously, there are more in college given the greater number of games throughout the season because of the large amount of teams. There are also some plays which end up being counted as fake attempts, although they were not designed that way, such as plays resulting from bad snaps. Out of the roughly 240 designed fake attempts, almost a third of them have come on fourth down and less than 3 yards to go. Obviously, that is the most popular time to attempt a traditional conversion as well. The chart below compares the success rate of fake attempts with the success rate of traditional attempts on fourth down based on the yardage needed to gain a first down.

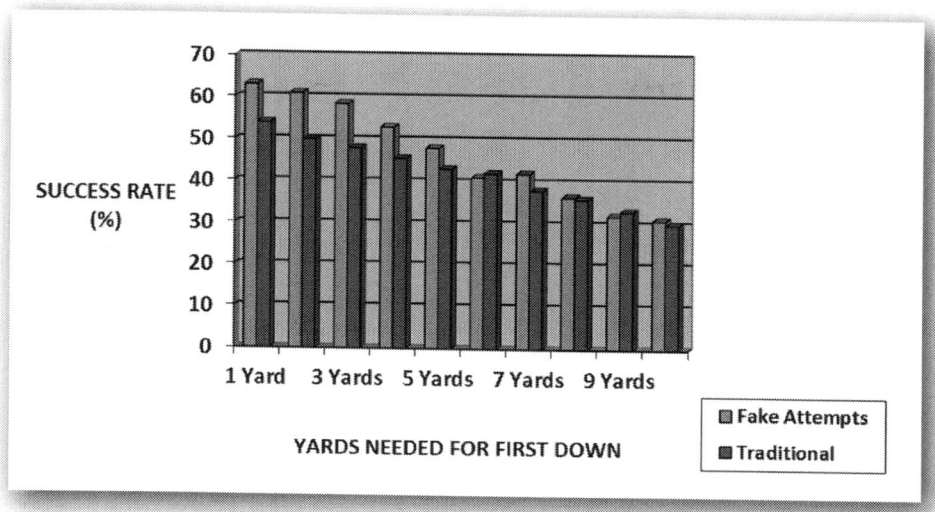

Based on the results of these attempts, it appears that fake plays have mostly outperformed traditional attempts; however, the difference between the two decreases as the yards necessary to achieve a first down increase. Obviously, the fake attempts rely on the surprise factor, in that the best time to run them is when the defense is not expecting them, just as we discussed with onside kicks. Additionally, many fakes are called when a coaching staff notices certain "tells," meaning that defenses are not defending against the fakes or have been leaving certain opportunities available for the offense to run a specific fake play. As of the time this book was written, it seems that fake attempts are more successful than they should be, but until the statistics revert to the mean, teams should be utilizing these plays more often when a defense does not seem to be expecting a fake attempt. Therefore, these plays should be called when the offense needs less than 5 yards to gain a first down and the defense is not expecting such a call, such as having incorrect personnel on the field or being setup in a formation not designed to stop such a play.

We are now going to briefly discuss squib kickoffs, which have become somewhat commonplace in the NFL. As most of you are aware, a squib kick is a low, line-drive kick that is meant to bounce before it is fielded by a receiver, thus resulting in a shorter return. These are typically used to keep the ball out of the hands of a skilled returner or to prevent a long return when the half or game is close to ending. Based on the statistics of the squib kick, if it is being used to run out the clock at the end of the game, a coach should be sure that either the clock will expire on the kickoff or that it will expire on the play after the kickoff. Therefore, there will typically need to be less than 12 to 15 seconds remaining on the clock prior to the kickoff in order to make the squib kick the proper decision. Otherwise, a normal kickoff as deep as possible will put the kicking team in the best position to protect a lead based on the average return at each level. When executing a squib kick, the kicker must also be sure to kick the ball deep enough to prevent the receiving team from having optimal starting field position.

For example, in 2008, the Chicago Bears were playing the Atlanta Falcons, and the Bears were leading 20–19 with 11 seconds remaining in the game and preparing to kick off. The Bears attempted a squib kick to prevent a long return but failed to kick the ball deep enough. As a result, the Falcons took over on their own 44 yard line. After a 26-yard completion, the Falcons ball carrier was able to get out-of-bounds with :01 remaining. The Falcons then set up and kicked a 48-yard field goal to win the game. Although there was poor defense played on the pass completion, a deep squib kick would have eliminated the possibility of that reception placing the Falcons in field goal range. However, it was executed incorrectly and not kicked deep enough, leaving the Falcons with much better field position and therefore a higher expected value, which ended up costing the Bears the game.

In Chapter 4, we covered fourth down decisions and when an offense should attempt a field goal versus their other options. The decision in that scenario was based on the average success rates of field goals as well as the expected value of such kicks based on the success rate. I have included two graphs below that show the average success rate of kickers in the NFL and NCAA for a coach's reference. This was intended to be a reference guide when determining whether to attempt a field goal. These statistics are based on the average kicker in ideal conditions. I did not include a high school graph because as we referenced before, high school kickers' skill levels vary so much, it could actually be counterproductive because such a graph would not be reliable. Instead, I recommend high school coaches develop their own tables based on the skill level of their particular kicker.

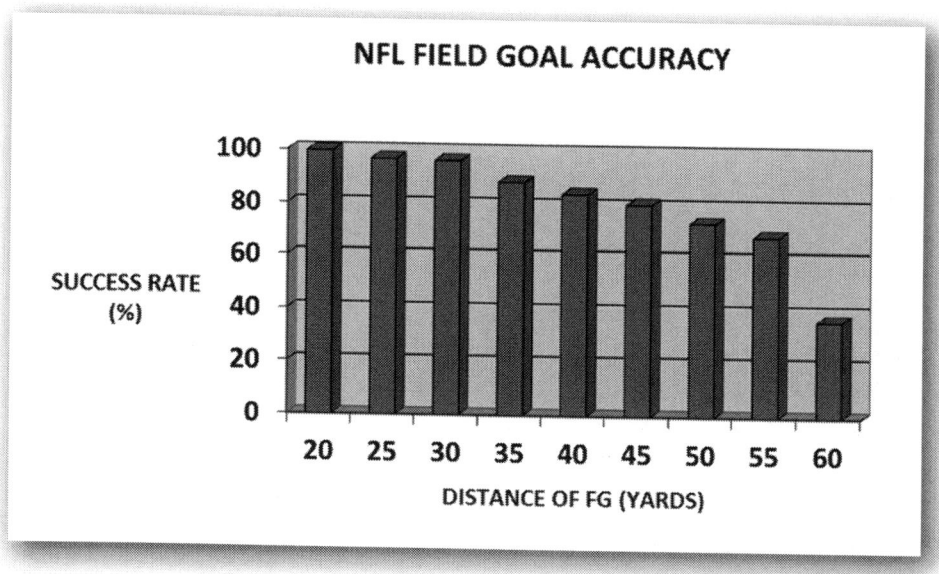

As you can see from the above graph, NFL kickers are very reliable on attempts that are 30 yards or less. On average, these accuracy numbers are about 20% higher than they were 30 years ago, because kickers have become much better over that period of time. As a result, the choice to attempt a field goal, especially outside of 50 yards, has become rather routine for coaches, whereas it was done a lot less frequently about 25 to 30 years ago. Let's now take a look at the same information for collegiate kickers.

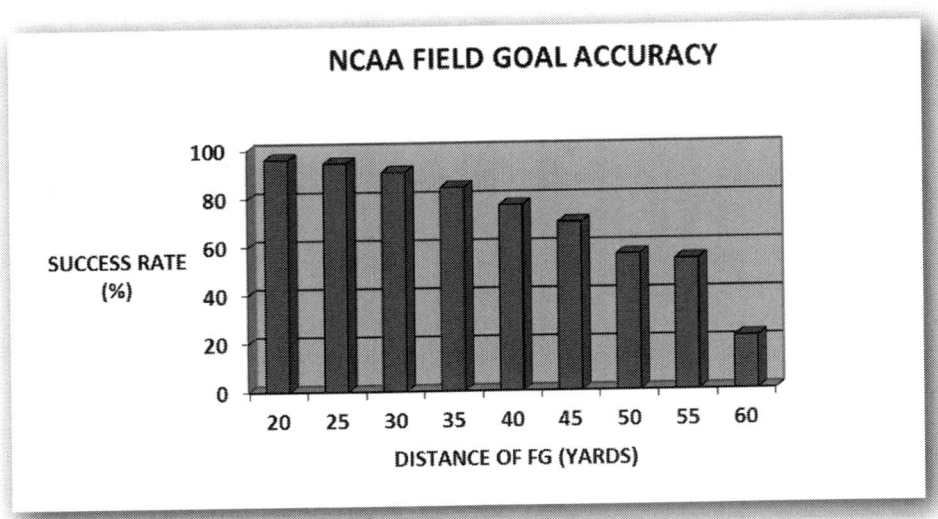

As you would expect, the percentages for successful kicks are slightly lower than the NFL statistics for corresponding distances. Again, these graphs are intended to be used as a reference point for coaches, and coaches must understand that it may be necessary to adjust this chart based on the strength and skills of each team's individual kicker. If an NFL or NCAA kicker's statistics vary significantly from the data in these charts, that could drastically change the expected value of a field goal as discussed in Chapter 4. As a result, it may be necessary to recalculate the figures of the fourth down decision chart in order to customize it for each team. When a team begins to implement the fourth down decision chart into their offensive game plan, every team should review it to make sure it is accurate and appropriate based on their players and averages.

In the following chapter, we are going to cover some information for coaches on incorporating some of the ideas introduced in this book. I will also offer some final thoughts and recommendations for coaches and play callers to consider when implementing the concepts and strategies previously discussed. For some coaches, it may be necessary to review this book or consult with their strategic coordinator every so often in order to ensure the principles are fresh in their minds and everyone is aware of the proper decisions to be made and the mechanics of doing so.

CHAPTER 6 SUMMARY

- Special teams have a correlation factor of approximately 18%, meaning that in an average game, special teams contribute about 18% to whether a team wins or loses that game.
- In the NFL, kickoffs that land in the end zone are relatively equally distributed as to how deep they travel into the end zone. In college, there are significantly less kickoffs that land greater than 6 yards deep in the end zone, likely due to reduced leg strength by the kicker.
- The majority of kickoffs returned from the end zone traveled less than 6 yards deep in the NFL and less than 5 yards deep in college football.
- The average starting field position resulting from a kickoff returned out of the end zone is relatively similar regardless of how deep in the end zone the returner fielded the kick.
- In the NFL, the expected value of returning a kick from the end zone is greater than the expected value of a touchback, accounting for penalties and turnovers, in almost every instance. In the case where this statement does not hold true, both expected values are equal, meaning there is no benefit to either decision.
- In college, the opposite is true, and the expected value of a touchback is generally greater than the expected value of a return from the end zone given that an offense's starting field position is at the 25 yard line after a touchback, as opposed to the 20 yard line in the NFL.
- Touchbacks have increased significantly since the location of the kickoff was changed in the NFL in 2011 and in college football in 2012.
- On average, punts are returned for a touchdown more often than kickoffs in both the NFL and college football; however, penalties are also more likely on punts at both levels.
- Factoring in the probability and expected value of a penalty or turnover, it is still beneficial for a defense to attempt to return a

punt, as opposed to signaling for a fair catch on each punt as recommended by some experts.

- Running a fake field goal or punt has been more successful than attempting a traditional play in order to gain a first down when the offense has less than 5 yards to gain for the first down and the defense is not expecting such a play.
- Squib kickoffs should only be used when the clock will expire on the kickoff or during the play immediately afterward. Squib kicks should travel sufficiently deep to avoid giving the receiving team quality field position.

Chapter 7

COACHES' SECTION

THE PURPOSE OF this chapter is to provide some additional information and suggestions to coaching staffs in order to assist them with understanding and implementing the concepts contained in this book. I understand that a lot of information has been covered, and it can be a bit overwhelming. However, this book does not have all the answers and solutions, but instead should serve as a foundation to provide the framework for proper clock management and other football strategies. As mentioned previously, employing all of the strategies contained herein can raise a team's winning percentage by almost 20% against a team not utilizing such strategies. Even if a coaching staff cannot or will not incorporate all of the recommended principles of this book, it is important to take small steps and incorporate certain strategies to increase a team's winning percentage, and hopefully, that same coach will be able to incrementally implement more and more concepts, which will only benefit their team. It is better for a coach to implement half or a portion of these strategies and increase their win probability by 8 or 10% than not implement any of the principles and miss out on an opportunity to earn an additional one to two wins per year.

These strategies should be used in every single game in which the team plays, not just the ones that are anticipated to be competitive. This way, both the coaches and players will become more familiar and confident with the decisions and be able to utilize the strategies without hesitation when needed. Additionally, a coach never knows when a "sure win" can turn into a back-and-forth struggle, so it is important to always implement these principles and concepts in order to provide the team with the best opportunity to win.

Again, it is important for a coaching staff to employ a strategic assistant to the head coach in order to assist with evaluations and calculations discussed previously. This individual will have the responsibility to not only review the concepts and calculations contained in this book but also understand the logic and statistical analysis behind them so that he can work with the coaches to implement the strategies properly. The strategic assistant must also be confident and thoroughly understand these strategies so he can communicate with the coaching staff as quickly as possible during game conditions.

It is also important for the assistant to have constant communication with the head coach and play caller, preferably through a headset, so he can communicate the appropriate calls and calculations to both of them. This coach need not be present at every team practice or meeting, but it is recommended that the assistant meet with the coaches prior to the season to discuss the implementation process and prepare certain plays to incorporate into the playbook. The strategic assistant can also provide drills to be incorporated in practices to help enforce these strategies. Additionally, the strategic assistant must be present at each and every game to provide the required information and calculation results to the head coach and play caller so they can make the appropriate decisions. He should also be responsible for communicating the proper pace to the quarterback during the game so the offense can operate according to the pace graph in Chapter 2.

In that chapter, I recommended that the offensive play caller have the plays divided according to pace. It is not necessary to have five different play sheets for the five different paces; however, I would suggest having at least three play sheets, one for quick paces (Paces Four and Five), one for an average pace (Pace Three), and one for a slow paces (Paces One and Two). Again, plays can appear on more than one play sheet if they fit the goals and objectives of two different paces, but having separate play sheets should make it easier and quicker for the play caller to determine what to call, especially when an offense is operating in Pace Four or Five and time is of the essence. It is also recommended that each play sheet be color-coded to allow for easy identification. I would also suggest having each play sheet with a certain background or border color corresponding to a traffic signal, which indicates the pace of that play sheet. For example, the quick pace play sheet could be color-coded in green, as in the offense should be moving at a quicker pace, such as vehicles at a green light. Similarly, the average pace could be identified by a yellow background or border, where the offense is not operating at either a slow or fast pace. Finally, the slow-paced offensive play calls can be coded in red, indicating a slowed or almost stopped pace.

Additionally, I would recommend that the strategic assistant have a corresponding color code to indicate to the play caller and quarterback the pace in which the offense should be operating. As I mentioned earlier, the assistant should be located on the field where he is visible to the necessary parties, and I have found that the best place is usually around 10 to 12 yards behind the line of scrimmage, which would separate him from many of the people standing at or near the line of scrimmage. The assistant would have a green wristband on his left wrist and a red wristband on his right wrist. When the previous play concludes, the assistant will indicate to the play caller and quarterback in what pace the offense should be operating by utilizing the color-coded wristbands. The left arm (green wristband) extended out to the side of the body at a 90-degree angle would indicate a Pace Five offense. Meanwhile, the left arm being extended straight up into the air toward the sky would indicate a Pace Four offense to the parties. If the offense should be in Pace Three, the assistant's arms would be crossed forming an "X" in front of the body, such as an intentional foul call in basketball. The right arm (red wristband) being extended straight up into the air would be Pace Two, and finally, the right arm being extended to the side of the body would be a Pace One offense.

This needs to be done by the assistant immediately after the conclusion of the previous play so the play caller and quarterback can understand the proper pace in which they should operate. Again, this is not necessary if the game clock is stopped between plays because the offense's pace would not mater at this point. This is why it is important to employ a proper assistant who understands the pace and calculations behind the concepts so he can quickly communicate them to others. Once the pace is indicated, the play caller will use the corresponding play sheet and signal or call the play to the quarterback. It is then the quarterback's job to communicate the play to the rest of the offense, whether it be in a huddle or otherwise. The quarterback's final responsibility is to get the offense set up and snap the ball at the proper time, depending on the current pace of the offense. As you can see, there are a lot of moving parts, so it is imperative that teams practice this process prior to the season starting so everyone is aware and can perform their responsibilities in a timely manner. Both the players and the coaches need to practice this process so that it can become second-nature when the games start. This is another reason I am surprised that teams do not use strategic assistants to help with the logistics.

In today's game, the head coach has so many other factors to consider and decisions to make, he cannot possibly consider all of the data and calculations we have discussed prior to making a decision within the 25- or 40-second play clock. Think about it: if a head coach did not have to worry about what pace an offense should operate in, when to call time-outs, when to attempt an onside kick or 2-point conversion, or what the proper call is on fourth down because he delegated the responsibility of considering the correct play based on statistical research to a strategic assistant, a head coach would have so much additional time to evaluate the players on the field and the "X's and O's" of the game. Even if a head coach is uncomfortable delegating all of this authority to an assistant because he prefers to have total control, he can still veto the decision of the assistant when he chooses to do so; however, at least he has the information and statistical analysis provided to him prior to making the call.

A coach should not worry about the defense stealing the assistant's hand signals either. If the opposition is smart enough and has employed their own assistant, they should understand and expect in what pace the offense should be operating. Even if they do not understand or adhere to the concepts in this book, it will give them no advantage to decode the offense's pace signals because a play caller should have many different plays within each pace. A smart defense will expect certain types of plays during the game anyway, such as more running plays in the second half when a team is leading or snapping the ball earlier in the play clock when a team is trailing.

An offensive play caller should have the playbook organized by types of plays as well. For example, late game lateral and Hail Mary plays as discussed in the Chapter 5 can be grouped in the same section. Additionally, similar plays such as medium passes to be used in a slow-paced offense can be grouped together as well. This will make it easier for the play caller to locate the appropriate play given the circumstances of the game and allow more time for the other moving parts between plays.

When a coach chooses to begin incorporating some or all of the principles contained in this book, the team should develop some clock management and strategic goals that they can track to measure the effectiveness of the incorporated concepts. I mentioned earlier that one of the easiest ones to track is effective possessions and the percentage of games in which each team has one more effective possession than their opposition. Teams should also track the fourth down decisions they make, specifically the percentage of the time they are successful attempting to convert a fourth down. This calculation can also notify a coach if more or different short yardage plays should be incorporated into the playbook.

Special teams coaches should also maintain the percentage of successful field goals converted and the distances of each attempt by the kicker to compare to the tables in the previous section. Offensive coaches should track when the ball is snapped while the offense is operating in a slow or fast pace. A team should aim to snap the ball at the appropriate time when the game clock is running at least 80% of the time. Coaches could also track how long it takes their offense to set up and snap the ball for a spike play or last-second field goal during a game and compare that to their timing in practice. Ideally, the strategic assistant could track all of these statistics and present the results to the head coach, but if there is not such an assistant, the coaches listed above should be recording this data for evaluation after each game.

One item that has not been addressed in this book is inclement weather, such as a strong north or south wind. Most coaches believe that when wind can affect the game, a team should want the wind at their back in the fourth quarter, but some coaches do not know why. Most believe this is the proper decision because games are often decided in the fourth quarter. While this concept can be true, there is a more tangible reason to have the wind at a team's back in the fourth quarter. Assuming there is an equal number of plays run in the first and third quarters, as well as in the second and fourth quarters, there would be no significant advantage for a team to have the wind at their back in the first and fourth quarters as most coaches choose, because the amount of plays run into and with the wind would be the same for both teams. However, this assumption is not entirely accurate.

Statistically, more plays are run in the fourth quarter than any other quarter because of the increased amount of time-outs utilized by both teams, the unique clock stoppage rules when the ball carrier travels out-of-bounds toward the end of the quarter, and the 2-minute warning in the NFL. Additionally, there is a greater chance of a team operating in Pace Four or Five in the fourth quarter, which would increase the number of plays being called as well. Therefore, if there is a strong north or south wind, and a team wins the coin toss before a game, it is important to defer and choose to have the wind behind them in the fourth quarter. If this is the case, you would want to increase the number of plays run in the first quarter as well, when the wind would also be at that team's back. This can be done by calling more pass plays, which will result in additional clock stoppages, and encouraging ball carriers to run out-of-bounds when possible to temporarily stop the game clock. Offenses should also operate in an increased pace during this period, which will increase the number of plays in the quarter as covered previously. The opposite would be true as well, and when a team is driving into to the wind, they should use more running plays, stay in bounds, and operate in a slower pace than usual in order to utilize more game time resulting in fewer plays being run in those quarters when the offense is at a disadvantage.

If there is not a significant wind or if the game is being played indoors, there is no real ascertainable advantage in choosing to defer or receive. Some coaches in the past have stated that they prefer to defer if they win the coin toss so they can have possession to start the second half when they have more information about the opponent. I do not believe that there is a significant advantage to implementing this theory. Nowadays, NCAA and NFL teams have so much game tape to review on opponents prior to the game that coaches should have all the information they need before the game even starts. If anything, I believe that there may be an advantage to receiving the kickoff in the first half. The reason behind this theory is rather simple. The only way a team can possibly have one more possession than their opponent in a game is to have the last effective possession of the half in which they have the first possession. As stated earlier, teams today do not properly plan to have the last possession of the first half like they should or like they often do in the second half. Near the end of the second half, teams start to realize the importance of having the last possession and begin proceeding accordingly. Therefore, if a team receives the kick to start the game and they plan properly according to the strategies discussed previously, it should be easier for a team to have the last effective possession of the first half as opposed to doing the same in the second half.

Well, that is all the information and analysis to be included in this edition of the book. Again, this is meant to provide the structure and framework for implementing the proper strategies, but in no way is it all-inclusive. There are many other concepts and principles that we did not cover in this book, but all coaches and strategic assistants should constantly be evaluating different aspects of the game and preparing the necessary calculations to determine the proper decision or course of action. I have included some of my contact information in the author biography section should anyone have any questions, concerns, or even simple comments.

CHAPTER 7 SUMMARY

- This book does not contain all of the relevant strategies that football teams should be implementing, but it should provide a good foundation on which to build. Utilizing the concepts and principles could improve a team's win probability by as much as 20%.
- Even if a team chooses to implement just a portion of these strategies covered in this book, they should practice them prior to the season and be prepared to use them in every game.
- Each team planning to use these concepts should employ a strategic assistant to the head coach to assist with the calculations and play calls. This will allow the head coach to focus more on evaluations and other football-related decisions, and he still has the opportunity to overrule the assistant if he chooses to do so.
- The play caller should have a color-coded play book based on the paces discussed previously in this book, and the assistant can use the corresponding colors to communicate the proper pace to the quarterback and play caller.
- Each team should work with the strategic assistant to develop goals to track and measure the effectiveness of clock management and other strategic decisions recommended in this book.
- When there is a strong north or south wind, the team winning the coin toss should choose to have the wind at their back in the fourth quarter because that is generally when the most plays are run.
- When a team is driving into a strong wind, they should operate in a slower pace to decrease the number of plays in the quarter, and when a team has the wind at their backs, they should operate in a quicker pace to increase the number of plays.
- There is typically no advantage to kicking or receiving when winning the coin toss prior to the game other than the small probability that receiving in the first half may provide slightly better odds that such a team has one more effective possession than their opponent.

GLOSSARY

Average Pace Graph – A table displaying the yards per minute that an offense must gain to reach its target point, and detailing the corresponding pace in which the offense must operate to gain the necessary yardage.

Clock Management – A concept in football whereby a team utilizes certain strategies, certain plays, or operates in a certain pace, relative to the time remaining on the game clock, in order to increase a team's win probability.

Effective Possession – An offensive football possession where a team has a reasonable chance to obtain a scoring opportunity.

Expected Value - The net point differential, or average value, team would expect to experience from a given football decision or situation if that decision was repeated the process an infinite number of times.

Fake Play – A play where the offense lines up in a special team formation, but attempt to gain a first down or touchdown in a deceptive or unorthodox manner.

Favorite – A team that is more likely to win a specific game based on the betting lines or other calculation.

Field Goal Accuracy Percentage – The percentage chance that a field goal will be successfully converted from a given distance in the field. This percentage will vary based on the skill level of a team's field goal kicker.

First Down Correlation – The relationship between a given down or play and the likelihood that it will eventually result in a first down for the offense.

First Down Probability - The percentage chance that an offense will gain a first down in a specific set of down based on the current situation.

Fourth Down Decision Chart – A chart utilized by coaches that displays whether a team should kick a field goal, punt, or go for a first down based on the calculated expected value of each option.

Free Kick – A play allowed in the National Football League and high school levels whereby a team can receive an untimed and undefended field goal attempt from the line of scrimmage immediately after a receiver fair catches a punt.

Hail Mary Play – A long forward pass into the end zone late in a game of half, typically out of desperation, with little chance for success.

Hail Mary Range – The area of the football field from which a quarterback's arm will allow him to throw a pass to the opponent's endzone.

Hook and Ladder Play – An offensive play where one receiver runs a hook route, and upon receiving the pass, laterals the ball to a nearby teammate who attempts to gain as much yardage as possible.

Hurry-Up Pace – When an offense is attempting to preserve game clock by snapping the ball to start a play quicker than usual from the conclusion of the last play.

Intentional Safety – A play where an offense takes a safety on purpose in order to utilize time or avoid a more damaging situation.

Kneel-Down Time – When the remaining amount of time on the game clock can be utilized by the offense by simply taking a knee on each remaining play. This calculation factors in the time remaining on the game clock and the number of timeouts of the defense.

Lateral Play – A play used by an offense, typically in desperation situations, whereby at least one lateral takes place. These plays are generally used as the last play of the game when the defense is located outside of Hail Mary range.

Loss Addition – A way of calculating which team is favored in a particular game where the amount of each team's previous opponents' losses are added to the current team's records, and the team with the highest winning percentage afterward is then considered the favorite.

Max Slow-Down – An offensive pace where the amount of time utilized by the offense is more important than whether they are able to score. This pace is used late in the game or half when the team leading is attempting to use the remaining time on the game clock to preserve the victory.

No-Huddle Offense – When an offense shortens or avoids a formal huddle between plays in order to disrupt defensive strategies or substitutions. This can be used as part of a hurry-up offense, but that is not always the case.

Normal Pace – A tempo in which an offense operates when they are not concerned with preserving or utilizing the game clock. Instead, the primary goal is simply to score as many points as possible.

Pace (Tempo) – The speed at which an offense is calling and executing their plays. It is measured by the amount of time between the conclusion of the previous play and the start of the subsequent play.

Play Sheet – A sheet used by coaches and coordinators listing the plays available to them to be called.

Pre-Snap Activities – Actions that take place before the snap for strategic or deception purposes, such as shifts, motion, audibles, etc.

Scoring Frequency – The average rate at which an offense scores points. It is usually calculated by dividing the number of game minutes played in a specific period by the total number of offensive scores during that same period.

Scoring Maximization – The process under which an offense attempts to score as many points as possible during a given drive or game.

Scoring Probability – The percentage chance that a specific offensive drive will result in a score given the current circumstances.

Slow-Down Pace – When an offense is operating at a pace where scoring is of primary importance, but utilizing game time is a secondary objective.

Squib Kick - A low, line-drive kickoff that is meant to bounce before it is fielded by a receiver, thus resulting in a shorter return. This type of kick is usually used in the final seconds of the half or game.

Strategic Assistant – An assistant coach who advises the head coach on clock management and other strategic decisions based on statistical analysis and calculations.

Target Point – The yard line on the field where an offense needs to gain in order to setup for a score to tie or win the game.

Touchback Percentage – The percentage of kickoffs that result in a touchback for a specific kicker.

Touchdown Probability – The percentage chance that a specific offensive drives results in a touchdown given the current circumstances.

Underdog - A team that is less likely to win a specific game based on the betting lines or other calculation.

Victory Point (see also Kneel Down Time) – The point in a football game when an offense is leading and can utilize the rest of the game time by simply taking a knee on each remaining play.

Win Correlation (Correlation Factor) – The relationship between a specific unit or player and the percentage chance of winning the game.

Win Probability – The percentage chance that a team will win a specific game at a given moment in time factoring in all of the circumstances affecting the game at that time.

Win Probability Calculator – A program that calculates the win probability at any point in a game given the applicable circumstances at that time.

Source/Reference List

Advanced NFL Stats. http://www.advancednflstats.com

Carroll, Bob; Palmer, Pete; & Thorn, John. (1988). *The Hidden Game of Football*. New York, NY: Warner Books.

Drive By Football. http://www.drivebyfootball.com

Elias Sports Bureau. http://www.esb.com.

ESPN. http://www.espn.com.

Minitab. http://blog.minitab.com

Reed, John T. (2010). *Football Clock Management*. Alamo, CA: John T. Reed.

Romer, David. (2006). Do Firms Maximize. *Journal of Political Economy*, 114(2), 340-365.

INDEX

Made in the USA
Charleston, SC
16 January 2016